All works are printed with permission from their original authors

All works copyright their original authors

Edited by Paul Tyng

Cover by Jenn Strunge

Thinking Beard Press – Baltimore - 2011

an earlier version of Packing/Pecking premiered in 2009 at the DC Source Festival

The Un Saddest Factory Presents

Ten Minute Play Festival

August 2011 – Volume 2

Table of Contents

Aldo is On the Floor 5

Dicey 12

Tide Pool 26

The Pelican Brief 37

A Funny Discussion 48

Shut the Front Door 55

Bem's Hypothesis 68

Packing/Pecking 77

Snowverdose 90

Nibs 107

Bath Time is Fun Time 121

Lone Drummer 137

Looking 145

Order 158

Aldo is On the Floor

by Megan McShea

CHARACTERS

MARCELLA: a middle-aged, beautiful woman who does not waste an ounce of energy on foolishness, doesn't get too agitated about anything in fact. Wizened, bemused, Marcella has lived a long time, which you can tell by the perfect orchestration of neck, shoulders, and my! those hands.

SOPHIE: a young woman with high aspirations who is very hard on herself for sport, always finding new reasons for beating up on herself. This is her idea of fun.

ALDO: a local fuckup who is tolerated by those around him because he is very earnest and can be very entertaining. He might have a black eye.

PIANO PLAYER: doing his job, keeping it light.

COMEDIAN: the opposite of Aldo: not entertaining, not earnest, a parasite, but a charmer.

THE SCENE

(A small cabaret, night. Everyone in the room is there for a good time, getting everything they can out of the brief leisure of the working class. There is a sense of levity, quickness, lightness, but everyone is also agitated in his or her own way.)

(Marcella and Sophie sit at a table together, leaning in towards each other. Sophie is whispering animatedly, but you can't hear her at first. She's aware of Aldo in that way pretty woman can sometimes be aware of men, fending off any potential attention by speaking quietly to Marcella. Aldo is at the next table, facing Marcella's back, alone with a bottle. Aldo can't help looking at Marcella, but he isn't talking to her. He is drunk enough to talk to himself without self-consciousness. His soliloquy is directed at some imaginary jury, as if he is on trial. He tries to deliver his defense with the charisma of a smooth attorney, but he is really too drunk. Marcella can't help listening to Aldo, but she isn't looking at him.)

ALDO

On the subject of the palette I have much to say, and it pleases me to do so. I will expound and contract like any ordinary caterpillar, earthworm, accordion. I have no shoes, so to speak. I will avenge.

(Marcella says nothing at all in response to Sophie, resisting her neediness, but Sophie doesn't notice and continues her intense but nearly silent monologue. Marcella shifts her body backwards a bit, curious to hear Aldo.)

ALDO

I cannot redeem you. I cannot redeem this fact, that recurring conclusion, the day, the sun. I cannot. There is no need to be sorry. I am not. If you are sorry, it will ruin us.

> (Marcella is suddenly aware of the melodrama in front of her (in Sophie) and behind her (in Aldo) and finds it hilarious. She begins to laugh without making any particular sound at all. It is by the perfect concerto of body language alone that one might know she is laughing. Sophie stops talking and widens her eyes at Marcella. She assumes she is laughing at Aldo. She kicks Marcella under the table and looks away, trying not to laugh herself.)

> (An image of cotton ball clouds dotting a blue sky is projected as large as possible on the entire set. It is everyone remembering the beautiful day, all at once, and disassociating from the present.)

ALL

> (sighing)

Ahh!

> (Aldo feels like a clown and forms the word buffoonery over and over again with his entire face.)

ALDO

B B B. foonery. Foonery. Buffoonery. Bu bu bu. But I am of no account. I am a no account.

> (Marcella finally turns to look at Aldo, like this: her head pivots quickly, smoothly, miraculously,

the way a squirrel will scale a tree, as if no time
had passed and it had never not been in the tree.
This graceful, simple gesture is like a physical
blow to Aldo. As if in a chain reaction, part of
one long fluid movement begun by Marcella's
head, Aldo's eyes roll back and his head rolls
back on his neck and his chair falls back. He tries
a backward somersault and lands on his side.)

ALDO

There's a story for you. In your teeth! In the nose! There's a story for you on your side on the floor. I am no story. I am a no account. A palette of perishable material.

(Fortunately for all, the piano player arrives for
work at this moment, takes off his coat, sits, and
begins to play, conveniently drawing focus from
Aldo's escalating debacle. The piano music can
be recorded, but the piano player should be
seated behind something that looks like a piano,
and we should be able to see his face. He
watches the goings on with detachment. For
music, I suggest Charlie's theme from Francois
Truffaut's "Shoot the Piano Player," or
something with a similar sound.)

(Sophie takes Marcella's hand and tries to draw
her back into conversation. Her thoughts are
varied and intense. Tonight she focuses on her
lack of knowledge of German history. Tomorrow
it will be something else. She is worried about
her lack of intellectual rigor, and with self-
dramatizing nihilism, wonders if it even
matters.)

SOPHIE

I do not know a single thing about German History before the last century. I do not know how Prussia fits into anything. Is it my fault I am confused on this point? Does it even matter that I am ignorant?

> (Sophie is the intense one of the conversation, and Marcella does not return the intensity. Marcella responds to Sophie as if she were following the movements of a tiny spider on the ceiling, as she often does when Sophie compels her to speak.)

MARCELLA

You are so impulsive, Sophie. You want to know everything. Germany indeed. History! There was a war, there is a war. We are here now and Aldo is on the floor. Thank God for the piano player. Some people are in jail. Have a drink.

> (Marcella refills Sophie's glass.)

ALDO

> (on the floor)

A veritable palette of perishable material!

> (lights dim.)

PIANO PLAYER

> (croons)

What was it you said that time

Under the stars so true If it wasn't for you I'd be so blue

> (During the song, the comedian comes on stage in the dark and stands before the microphone. The spotlight has not yet come on, but Marcella

is sitting close and watches him. His eyes meet
hers and he opens his mouth slowly, slowly
wider as if he were about to eat the microphone
in one bite. Suddenly a spotlight comes on and
the comedian begins his routine. This comedian
and his routine may be simply a memory of
Marcella's – like the clouds. Nobody reacts to
the comedian's presence except for Marcella.
She liked the comedian in the dark, with his
open, silent mouth, but she gradually sours on
him as he begins his routine. He is clearly kind
of an ass.)

COMEDIAN

You are Germany indeed. History is on the floor. Thank God for the war. We are now the piano player and Aldo is in jail. Some people want to know everything. Have a drink, Sophie!

(Canned laughter.)

MARCELLA

One cannot know everything.

COMEDIAN

A drink! A drink!

(Aldo stands suddenly, directly in the
comedian's spotlight. Aldo, in a gesture of self-
composure, tightens his belt by one hole.
Marcella brightens at this. Policemen come and
quietly arrest Aldo. The comedian exits, having
lost his audience during the arrest. The spectacle
over, everyone looks at the piano player, who
plays throughout.)

MARCELLA

Little puffs of clouds, like cotton balls, all afternoon.

PIANO PLAYER

(sings)

What was that you said,

If not tonight Then you might To my delight Another night?

(Sophie returns to her rant.)

SOPHIE

Nineteenth century German history is a complete blind spot.

MARCELLA

(suddenly remembering)

I passed Aldo on the street once, and we talked about the clouds.

(lights fade and the piano plays on. The end)

Dicey

by Mason Ross

This story takes place during a role-playing session. One person (Allison), is the Dungeon Master (also referred to as a Game Master). It is the DM's job (or GM's job) to tell the whole of the story. Allison is in charge of everything in the game. She sets the stage and plays every character except for three of them. Alan, Sam, and Carlo decide the actions of one character apiece. This is what a role playing game is. Communal story telling. Four complete nerds sit around a table. On the table sits some papers, some dice, some miniatures, and an open box of pizza. There is also the quintessential mountain dew. Perhaps these are not there, perhaps the nerd-dom will not be the thing highlighted. Whatever. What is important is the map of the fictional world of Casia in the background. It is big enough for the audience to see, Allison made it, and it is impressive, both in its execution and the nerdiness that it required. Allison points to continents and locations on it throughout the first scene. It is definitely there. So are the books. Some books are somewhere there. Maybe there is some other nerdy shit elsewhere in the room. Again, whatever.

In general, feel free to ignore my stage directions.

CHARACTERS

ALLISON (AL): Known as "Al" throughout the script, dresses in very plain and comfortable clothing. It takes place in her house and she is wearing what she would be wearing if this Sunday had instead been spent watching dumb television with her husband. This comfortablilty in her dress and surroundings produce a genuine, raw, and honest sex appeal. These people are her closest friends. Her story telling skills are astounding. She is quick witted, alert, good at voices, and mesmerizing. She will gladly stand up and run around the room if she needs to. She is into this. It is fun.

ALAN: That guy that you know. He likes flannel. He knows new music, but listens to the same stuff that he did in high school. He is very calm, knows himself very well, he is funny, but not loud. He is the dream player to role-play with. He understands that the story is the most important thing and won't do anything to monkey wrench it. I love him.

SAM: The pretentious nerd. All of his t-shirts point to some at least fairly obscure nerdy reference. In the world of role playing there is a term called "Rules Lawyer." It defines a person who will argue with the Game Master in an attempt to promote their own personal gain. A Rules Lawyer's arsenal in argument consists of everything. Sam is that guy. This is his life. Gaming. He knows more than you. These three people are his best friends.

CARLO: He has no other friends. He dresses Target hip. He has probably brought beer. He is not here for the game. He is here because he, like everyone else playing the game used to feel when they were younger, has nowhere else to go where he feels accepted.

SCENE ONE

(Lights up)

AL

Let's begin

(stands, addresses map)

A recap.

> (She is SO into this)

Casia stands on the brink of a global war! Over the past year, its inhabitants have become increasingly aware that a seemingly astounding number of the planet's varied and various religions and politics are spearheaded by a network of underground secret organizations. The Elves of Alantarin

> (points to continent inhabited be elves)

have nationally renounced their once unifying faith after the prophet Rel returned from the grave and spoke out against the church's ancient mandate to rid the world of all Orc kind!

> (Points to part of continent inhabited be Orc's)

The Orc's on the other hand, have recently learned that all of their leaders were actually-

CARLO

You are so hot.

AL

> (Allison allows /forces herself to find this funny. We're all friends here)

I'm also married.

ALAN

> (Genuinely and sarcastically adoring AL, perhaps sighing)

We know that.

SAM

If you're already going to start interrupting her we'll never get started.

CARLO

Why doesn't Brad play?

AL

It's not his thing.

CARLO

I like Brad

(Beat)

I wasn't hitting on you.

AL

I know.

CARLO

Not really.

AL

I know.

SAM

Allison, you are forgetting rule number five.

AL

I know, don't respond to anything out of game that Carlo says.

CARLO

(He is tired of hearing that)

That's not a real rule.

SAM

(Wistfully)

It's real if we want it to be, but we have to really want it. Carlo, shut up, seriously.

ALAN

Yes. Carlo, you should stop interrupting Al so she can continue to accidently be super hot while the excruciatingly rare shimmering lights of nerd queendom cascade from her lips onto the canvases of our minds, painting the potential fate of her fictitious world.

AL

Ew.

ALAN

We all have our talents.

AL

(Her stride has not been in any way compromised. She is miming shit like crazy)

You find yourselves in an era where no one knows who to trust. The dark lord Keldon

(points towards Keldon's land, maybe she even has a drawing of the Dark Lord himself)

having amassed his own civilization of undead over a countless number of centuries saw, in this state of global upheaval, his opportunity to strike out against the races who have forever plagued his morbid enterprise. Keldon wants to kill the world and raise it from the dead in his image. His armada bleeds into the seas at this very moment, his influence seeping into the hearts and minds of everything that breathes. But, this party needs no reminder of Keldon and his endeavors. Galdric Baldlain

    (points to Alan)

the noble dwarven cleric, whose royal title of Prince was stripped from him after an ancient tablet was found disclaiming the ancient story of Kald-rak-roon, the fabled hammer that his lineage was based on. The ancient tablet said that Galdric's ancestors were in fact-

    ALAN

    (Alan's voice now sounds more like Galdric's)

Need we go over it again.

    AL

    (More deity like now)

Perhaps not... Raijin, the stoic monk

    (pointing to Sam)

whose long lost sister was last reported to be a slave aboard a merchant vessel. A merchant vessel known to illegally trade with Keldon's population of the undead. The ship, The Cormorant, never returned from its last voyage to Keldon's continent of the damned.

    SAM

    (Pure Raijin)

She has not fallen to him or to any other perilous fate, I have seen her in my dreams. We will be reunited over the corpse of

Keldon's tyranny.

>   AL

And the great and mighty amazon, Thorn, who-

>   CARLO

>   (Classic Thorn, am I right?)

Is in it for the money.

>   AL

Perhaps she is. But, perhaps the story will take a more dramatic turn for our fair amazon? Will her resilience to emotion be tested? Will she be forced to act not out of personal gain, but out of moral obligation? Let us begin, gentlemen. Roll for initiative.

>   (Lights down.)

SCENE TWO

>   (The set is clear. The actors are
>   now acting as their characters'
>   characters. Raijin holds a torch.
>   It is dim in this dark place our
>   party has found their way into.
>   The party enters in a line, slowly.
>   They are looking around a lot,
>   sounds are creepy and deadly
>   here. Allison is playing a
>   mutilated gnome. Perhaps this
>   gnome is also holding a torch. I
>   want Carlo to be in hot drag as
>   Thorn, but whatever.)
>
>   (Lights up.)

AL

(As a mutilated gnome)

I hear things here in the tunnels, but I do not see them. Do not be afraid. I travel alone though. The other times, when I am alone. When I don't see the things that make the noises. The things that I don't see. The things that I hear. Oh, the things that I hear. But, I am alone then. Now is different. I must be brave. We must be brave. I will run if there is trouble.

CARLO

You will run no where, gnome! You will take us where we have paid you to take us! And if trouble arises you will not leave us here to die!

SAM

Might I suggest that we continue in silence, fair amazon. I do not wish to disturb any sub-terranean beasts at this point in our journey.

ALAN

The monk is right. Guide, continue, but please-

AL

Shh... A stranger approaches.

ALAN

(listens)

He's right, I hear it too. Ready your weapons, I'm going to bring some light to this dark place!

> (Galdric produces some items out of a pouch. He says some whispers.)

>> (STAGE LIGHTS TURN ALL THE WAY UP)

> (Looking around in fear and astonishment)

> (some beats)

Dear, Moradin!

SAM

(Truly terrified by what he now sees)

Galdric? I think you should undo your spell. I don't think they seem to particularly enjoy the light you have brought to this place.

ALAN

Right.

>> (Lights Down!)

SCENE THREE

>> (Everyone is back around the table again. They are playing the game and casually speaking in character.)

> (Lights up.)

AL

Your ship pulls into the elven port of Alantarin. Your Captain informs the three of you that he will wait at the docks for your return for as long as it takes, but reminds you that you must make haste, the window of opportunity is very short.

ALAN

Shall we enter the city?

>   (Sam and Carlo both give positive answers)

AL

You have arrived to Alantarin during a great festival it appears, you see many people standing around at the end of the docks-

ALAN

Uh-oh.

AL

You guessed it. The crowd sees you and cheers your names. There are fireworks and banners. You hear a band playing some sort of welcoming fanfare.

CARLO

I push pass them and find the nearest tavern.

ALAN

I attempt to sneak away. Can I roll to see if I successfully sneak away?

AL

It is too late. She has seen you . The young fair princess Anastalla is running to you, arms outstretched.

SAM

I'll be right here for you, Galdric, you have to let her down easy.

>   (The lights go quickly out. They
>   come up and Allison and Alan are

standing in an embrace, front and center.)

AL

Oh my little dwarf, how I hate it when you leave.

ALAN

(Sweetly)

My people do not typically enjoy being called little, your highness.

AL

And I do not appreciate all this "your highness" this and "your highness" that. You have been acting like you barely know me since the moment your ship landed.

ALAN

I'm sorry, Anastalla... I have something I need to say to you.

AL

No.

ALAN

What?

AL

No. I know where this is going. And you can't do this to me. I have been watching the horizon for days, waiting to see your ship and now that you're here you are mine. Even if just for a little while

(begins crying).

ALAN

I can't do that. I can't come here and have some sort of fantasy holiday with you. Come here and pretend that everything is okay? No. It is not okay. Everything is not okay.

AL

Don't you think I know that!?

ALAN

That's just it, Anas! I know that you do! You are just as aware as I am of what's going on here! You don't love me anymore either! Why are you pretending to?

AL

How dare you, you awful, little man? Of course I still love you. I will always love you.

ALAN

I think it would be easier if you hated me, your higneess.

(Breaking)

Allison, can we stop, I have to pee.

SCENE FOUR

(Allison sits alone on stage. She is talking on a phone. The scene is dressed very office building. Whatever you can add to make it seem more like "office building.")

(Lights up.)

AL

(Fast and monotone)

Can we get the boxes over to the building? Good. I was hoping that we could. I think they need to be there by noon on Monday. Things need to be put into the boxes by a certain time. Then, the boxes, now with the certain things in them, will be mailed to building number two. I believe they have to be there by the next day, which would be tuesday. The boxes should all be the same size and not wet. We can not use wet boxes. The wetness causes them to become less usable and therefore not as good. If it is raining when they are brought into the building there will be a higher chance of them getting wet, so people will need to be extra careful under such conditions. Please have back up boxes set aside in case something happens and I need to call you to get more boxes. If we don't get the boxes to building number two on time, they will have to wait to get them until they get there, which has not been the agreed arrangement. Thank you for your time. The Dark Lord Keldon is not as bad as he seems. Busy. Bye. Have a good day.

> (Lights down.)
>
> (Lights up on ALAN, SAM, and CARLO watching television. The anchor is describing a Giant Monster that is destroying Baltimore. It is somehow their fault. The players are terrified.)
>
> (Lights down.)
>
> (Lights up.)
>
> (CARLO eats pizza while dying. ALAN stands praying. SAM kneels over CARLO. ALLISON lies dead and bloody with a weapon in her chest. Horrible news reports and gunshots can be heard in the background.)

SAM

Go softly, sweet warrior. The world crumbles around us now. We will all be sleeping soon.

CARLO

Raijin, I want you to have all of my possessions... And I'm going to write up a new character soon and if you could give them my stuff-

SAM

She is speaking gibberish now, Galdric. It won't be long.

ALAN

See her off with that song she loves, Raijin, she wants to hear it, though she has not the heart to ask.

> (Sam sings the song Day-O. Carlo actually dies.)
>
> (Lights down.)

Tide Pool

by Lola B. Pierson

Scene 1

> Stage left is a small table with a radio on it. Stage right is a chest of drawers of trunk or something that contains all of the most special things. The stage is covered to some degree with scattered rocks and stones
>
> The Chorus can take basically any form. It can be a prerecorded voice over, it could be a live voice over, it could be live actors, or it could be some combination of the three. It can be one voice or many.
>
> There should be a distinct switch in Eel when she is speaking to The Radio, specifically she should be thoroughly engaged as those all of those scenes are actually taking place with a lover.
>
> The Radio can take many forms.

EEL

There is the numbness of white haze. I cannot sleep after long days. No, not that. That was a terrible beginning.

CHORUS

Start over.

(She exits. Re-Enters.)

EEL

Everything you see before you was once the moon.

> (She pauses, waits for a response and, hearing none, continues.)

That was too formal, maybe.

> (She stays motionless for a second. Maybe has a brief non-verbal interaction with the audience, maybe. Another pause.)

CHORUS

You have to do something.

EEL

You mean that uh...? Well, never mind.

CHORUS

"Never." "Mind." Used to suggest that a problem or objection is not important.

> (Pause)

You should tell a story about a gorilla and a baby.

EEL

It gets less sad every time I say it out loud. Every time it makes someone else sad it makes me a little less sad. Soon it will not make me sad at all and the whole wide world will be weeping.

CHORUS

You would have to act it out because neither one of them could talk.

EEL

I fell in love with the moon.

> (She walks over to the radio and turns it on. Switches through several stations until she gets to the "water station" which is just a radio station that plays only water sounds. Like the ocean. She finds this comforting and leans against something, then slowly slides down so that her head is right near the radio.)

CHORUS

You have to do something.

> (EEL wakes, as if from a dream, stands, speaks to the audience.)

EEL

We spent the whole season at the beach that summer, or maybe it was some other year, I can't remember now. From Earth we always see the same side of the moon, the other side is always hidden from our view. Even so...still.

CHORUS

"Still." Up to and including the present or the time mentioned; even now.

EEL

I feel in love with the moon that summer and I still remember exactly how it happened.

> (She walks over to the radio, switches the channel to the "Memory Station.")

THE RADIO

I never met anyone like you before in my whole life.

EEL

(To the radio)

You make me feel like anything is possible.

THE RADIO

I think that I'm falling in love with you.

EEL

You're the best one.

THE RADIO

I like everything about you.

EEL

I love you exactly the way you are.

CHORUS

Is this happening now or is this what happened before?

EEL

All things are happening all at once if you really think about it.

CHORUS

That is a completely useless piece of information.

EEL

General information.

CHORUS

What?

EEL

You know like, "what time does the library close?" and "all things are happening at once," and also, "you make my heart beat out of my chest."

CHORUS

The last one.

EEL

What?

CHORUS

The last one isn't general information.

EEL

Maybe it just feels that way now. Classifiable data.

THE RADIO

You make my heart beat out of my chest.

EEL

(To The Radio)

The way I feel about you...it is almost unbearable.

THE RADIO

I want to hold your small shoulders, one in each hand. I want to smell you and feel the small of your back.

> (As he says this Eel acts it out. She's basically making out alone. This can be very non-realistic, even hyper exaggerated like a dance.)

Your teeth are small, I want to touch them while I pull your hair. I want to rub your face gently as your head rolls back and your eyes lose focus.

(Eel finishes and reaches stillness.)

EEL

Still.

CHORUS

"Still" Not moving or making a sound. Or as a noun: deep silence and calm: stillness.

EEL

(Stands, addresses the audience.)

Oh, never mind.

CHORUS

"Never mind." Used to indicate that what has been said of one thing applies even more to another: as in he was so tired that he found it hard to think, never mind talk.

EEL

(To the audience)

The moon and I fell in love and I knew we were forever. I had never known that kind of thing before, but there was something about this time that I just knew. And he would say things, things like

THE RADIO

I want to start a family with you.

EEL

And I knew that The Moon knew we were forever too. That this moon was mine, that I could finally be happy. That you can be happy forever as long as you don't expect to be happy every second. At the end of every day we could sit and look at each other and still be in love.

> (We hear three ticks.)

CHORUS

The time.

EEL

And then

> (Silence)

The eclipse. The moon went away. He...was gone. And I liked the fact that he was always changing, I did. It was a thing I loved about him. It was a thing I understood that most people didn't. And when, the darkness...people acted like I should've known. People acted like it was no big deal because they knew it was coming. Like something is made less horrible by knowing about it in advance. And anyway I didn't know about it in advance. People said

THE RADIO

It was in the paper.

EEL

People said

THE RADIO

You never pay attention so you never know what's going on.

EEL

People said

THE RADIO

It's just the Earth aligning with the Sun that's casting a shadow over the moon.

EEL

Which made me feel like I had crumbled up paper in my stomach. When I was little our dog got hit by a car and afterwards, afterwards my friend Gretchen Weiner from school who had seen the whole thing called me on the phone and told me what it looked like. And it lasted forever.

>(Pause, a switch)

>(She looks around the stage.)

If I had a phone I could wait for him to call. Did you know-did you know that three wars have been started by eclipses? The wait. Is what expands time. Elongates. Special relativity or general relativity?

CHORUS

What?

EEL

It's a science joke.

CHORUS

It's not a very funny one. It doesn't play very well.

EEL

"Never mind."

CHORUS

Used in refusing to answer a question: never mind where I'm going.

EEL

And then...he came back. But he was different. It was different now. And he only looked vaguely familiar so I asked him straight out. I said, "you look vaguely familiar. did we get married and have three children once?"

THE RADIO

You know when you make the private public it loses meaning.

EEL

I tried to write you a letter for every day you were gone.

> (She walks to the container of all the most special things and pulls out a number of half written letters. There should be at least 50.)

But I got tired of it. Or maybe I realized that I am just not that kind of person.

> (Pause)

You forgot.

THE RADIO

I just don't want to be inauthentic.

EEL

You say that every time.

THE RADIO

I know, but this time I really, really mean it.

EEL

Oh. Well in that case…

(She doesn't move.)

THE RADIO

I wish I could honestly say that the way I wish it was was the way it was.

(Quickly)

I think it was always this way and we never really loved each other and that's okay I hope we can still be friends.

EEL

Later The Moon would tell me that I was just seeing things differently. That he has actually stayed the same the whole time. That my position had changed, not his. That he had been the same all along.

CHORUS

You have to do something.

EEL

I wanted to be near the motion of the water. He said we would go swimming out past the waves and the the waters would be calm, but I didn't understand that as I have never seen the ocean.

CHORUS

Share something deep and dark.

EEL

There is no such thing as privacy.

CHORUS

Share something deep and dark and personal.

EEL

There is no such thing as privacy for someone like me.

CHORUS

Share something deep and dark and personal and accessible.

EEL

There is nothing left.

CHORUS

Share something deep and dark and personal and accessible and surprising.

>(Eel walks over to the radio. Turns it up loud! The Moon explodes. Eel lies down center stage with her head facing out, eyes open. She is frozen. Probably dead. Blackout.)

The Pelican Brief

by Josh Van Horne

PROSECUTION

Ladies and Gentleman of the jury, I am here before you today to expose famed entrepreneur and Aquarius, Stubly Mangrove as a depraved and craven philanthropist

(Audience gasps)

PROSECUTION

On August 27, 1993, Mangrove was attending a Mooshball match in Pomegranate Town when he got into an argument with Laura the Labcoat, Pomegranate Town's star Moosh Ball player and most specialized garment.

DEFENSE

Objection your honor! Laura the Labcoat was never the star player. She will always play second yodel to Tommy Teammate.

JUDGE

Objection... acknowledged. Tommy is a favorite of Mooshball enthusiasts the world around. Laura was notoriously inept when defending against a 15 Gravut Brainbow.

PROSECUTION

IRREGARDLESS! Mangrove was arguing with Laura the Labcoat when a scream was heard in the halls of the Pomegranate Town Mayor's Office, several miles away. When the Mooshball match finally ended, the mayor discovered the body of his best friend, Laura the Labcoat, brutally philanthropized in the vestibule of his house, the Mayor's Office.

JUDGE

You tell a compelling story, if I had to verdictify right now I would rule in your favor. Unfortunately the defense has yet to speak, so let's give them a listen.

DEFENSE

Your honey, my client, Stubly Mangrove, did not philanthropize Laura the Labcoat. In fact, contrary to popular belief, Stubly Mangrove has never engaged in philanthropy. Sure, he's dabbled in Volunteerism and for a time in college he experimented with benevolence, but those wild days are in the past. Stubly is a model citizen. He drives a car, he eats food tri-daily, and he votes republican, democrat or independent. Today, we will set the record straight!

JUDGE

I am tickled pink by your spirited and incredibly articulate defense. Prosecution, the mooshball is in your corpundery.

PROSECUTION

Thank you, your honor. The prosecution would like to call its first witness to the stand, Jomythym Mogtomery.

(Enter Jomythym - rhymes with Jonathan)

PROSECUTION

Jomythym, where were you on the night of Laura the Labcoat's philanthropization?

JOMYTHYM

I was away on a business trip with my kids at a teleconference about the interview.

(Audience gasps)

PROSECUTION

Thank you – the Prosecution rests.

JUDGE

Defense, the witness is all yours.

DEFENSE

Jomythym, do you know?

JOMYTHYM

Yes.

DEFENSE

Stenographer, let the record show, he knows. Jomythym, can you descend please.

(Jomythym descends from the witness stand. Saunters.)

JUDGE

Somebody call Levi's Jeans because this is a riveting display.

> (Prosecution repeatedly taps wine glass with a fork)

PROSECUTION

Your honor, it would be a pleasure to call the next witness to the stand, a very special lady who I'm sure WE ALL KNOW AND LOVE, Laura the Labcoat!

JUDGE

Hooray for scientific outerwear!

PROSECUTION

Hip hip! Hooray!

(Audience will most certainly exchange high fives at this point.)

(Enter Laura)

LAURA THE LABCOAT

Hello All. It is me, Laura the Laurora Borealis, I am exuberant that soon justice will be served and at long last I will get to tell my side of the story.

PROSECUTION

Exactly, justice is imminent!

LAURA

Now go ahead, asked, me ask me a question.

PROSECUTION

I'm revvin' up!

LAURA

Get that engine started!

PROSECUTION

Here I go!

LAURA

Go on!

PROSECUTION

OK! Laura, where were you on the night you were philanthropized at the Mayor's house, the Mayor's office?

LAURA

I was at Pomegranate Town's Sportsball Stadium, playing second yodel in a rousing Mooshball match when my friend and life partner, Stoffalus the Stunningly Attractive Stack of Stuff went to get a drink of water. Three weeks later we found his body laying face down at the Pomegranate Town Water Treatment Facility. He had been murdered in cold blood.

PROSECUTION

Do you need a tissue?

LAURA

No

DEFENSE

I would like one!

JUDGE

Me too!

> (Judge and defense tape the tissues to their faces.)

JUDGE

Continue.

LAURA

Once I found the corpse of my acquaintance Stoffalus, Stubly Mangrove rushed over, gave me a hug and offered to buy me a snack. I was flabbergasted.

PROSECUTION

Why is that?

LAURA

Gosh Darble Prosecution! Do I have to spell it out for you? He was openly engaging in philanthropy!

PROSECUTION

Can you elaborate?

LAURA

Yes – Stubly knows fully well that unsolicited offers of snacks are in violation of town ordinances. He's a philanthropist!

PROSECUTION

Thank you Ms. Labcoat. Defense, the witness is all yours.

DEFENSE

Laura the Labcoat, or SHOULD I SAY BROMWERTH P. HERBERDERFER THE BOURGEOISE MURDERER?

(Audience gasps)

LAURA

I prefer Laura the Labcoat.

DEFENSE

Just checking. Ms. Labcoat on scale of 1 to 10, how would you describe the generosity of my client, Stubly Mangrove?

LAURA

He's very generous. Often I find myself saying, "Here comes that generous old coot Stubly Mangrove, undoubtedly he comes with the intention of spreading joy and good spirits throughout the land."

DEFENSE

You say that every time you see him?

(Audience worriedly chatters)

LAURA

Every time.

> (Audience explodes metaphorically)

JUDGE

THERE WILL BE ORDER IN THE COURT!

DEFENSE

And how does Stubly respond?

LAURA

> (In Stubly's voice)

Well, hello Laura the Labcoat, it is I, Stubly Mangrove, a renowned practitioner of generosity and symbolic representation of the human condition.

DEFENSE

Objection your honor!

JUDGE

Tell it to the judge!

LAURA

He's truly abhorrent. I've never met a more despicable ambassador of all things human condition.

DEFENSE

Thank you Laura, here's a tissue.

LAURA

Thank you.

> (Laura affixes tissue to face)

JUDGE

Are there any more witnesses that either of you chabucklers would like to call to the stand?

DEFENSE

Yes, I would like to call Stubly Mangrove to the stand.

JUDGE

Is that OK with you, Prosecution team?

PROSECUTION

Make it so!

> (Enter Stubly Mangrove)

LAURA

Here comes that generous old coot Stubly Mangrove, undoubtedly he comes with the intention of spreading joy and good spirits throughout the land.

STUBLY

Well, hello Laura the Labcoat, it is I, Stubly Mangrove, a renowned practitioner of generosity and symbolic representation of the human condition.

> (Laura leaves the stand, Stubly replaces him on the stand.)

DEFENSE

Stubly, thank you for joining us on this blessed afternoon.

STUBLY

I was legally compelled to attend.

DEFENSE

Stubly, this is not the first time I've defended you, can you explain to the court your criminal exploits of the past 15 years.

STUBLY

Many of you might recall the time I poisoned the town's water supply and subsequently killed Stoffalus the Stunningly Attractive Stack of Stuff because he witnessed me poisoning the water supply.

PROSECUTION

Ah yes, who could forget that one.

STUBLY

Or how about the time I kidnapped Tommy Teammate and imprisoned him for 9 years because his Mooshball talents caused me to lose a bet worth several doubloons.

JUDGE

He remains in your compound to this day?

STUBLY

TO THIS VERY DAY HE REMAINS!

JUDGE

It is not necessary to yell Stubly.

STUBLY

Well if you recall that, then you might not be shocked to find out that I have also taken part in the most heinous crime of them all, philanthropy.

DEFENSE

YOU DASTARDLY BEING!

STUBLY

And I don't regret it one bit. When you volunteer, you're not just teaching a person to fish, you're teaching a village to raise a child. And that child will grow up and sentimentally look back on that time the whole village tried to raise them and with a twinkle in their eye they'll turn to you after you've finished volunteering, or you're on break from volunteering and they'll say in their most sentimental and heartfelt voice possible, "Thanks for being a part of that village, the one that helped raise me even though it violates town ordinances."

JUDGE

Nonsense. I will not allow you to fertilize this courtroom with such horse hockey.

STUBLY

Fair enough, it was a weak argument. But let me ask you this, your honor, do you remember the day you were born?

JUDGE

Of course.

STUBLY

And do you remember what the doctor said to your mother upon witnessing the miracle of your birth?

JUDGE

(Stuttering)

Y...y...yes, alas, I can hear it quite vividly.

STUBLY

Please elaborate.

JUDGE

I cannot, I'm afraid it shall impugn my already fragile reputation.

STUBLY

That it might, but as the old saying goes, "If a judge has something to say that could change the outcome of the trial, they should say it and then regret it later when they're incarcerated."

JUDGE

The adage is correct. I must be courageous.

STUBLY

Now Judge, what did the doctor say?

JUDGE

(In a doctor's voice)

Ma'am, this beautiful child is a gift to humankind!

STUBLY

A gift! Now, correct me if I'm wrong, I'm just a city boy, after all, but a gift sounds awfully like philanthropy.

JUDGE

(Sobbing)

Oh Jeepers! I'm a criminal.

STUBLY

That does it! Prosecution, arrest the judge at once! I declare myself, not guilty!

> (Victorious music, hugs are exchanged, 15 second dance routine involving entire cast and lighting crew.)

A Funny Discussion

by Theresa Columbus

CHARACTERS

PALASHA and BEDWA: Basically the same character distributed among two characters. This gives the actors and director some freedom to create a relationship between them that fluctuates. Gender is up in the air, though stage directions are written as though Palasha is female and Bedwa is male. It is important that there is not a cut and dry dynamic throughout, where one character is clearly the stronger, grumpier, etc. Each of these characters has a range of attitudes, but the attitude is generally sincere, not sarcastic.

The backdrop is a series of 2 dimensional shapes in various colors (without patterns) on a flat back wall with strange color combinations such as shades of maroon, red, purple, light blue and yellow. These shapes stand for shapes, stand for color, stand for symbols, but should not really look like art on the wall, nor should they look like wallpaper, or 80s geometric wall designs. They may take on a look of generic abstract theater backdrop. Set pieces and smaller objects ("props") upon the set pieces reflect these simple shapes with a slightly different color palette but a similar non-art/ sculpture feeling. These are barely noticeable on the side of the stage until they are brought out later in the play. The light on the stage starts out dim and then becomes gold and white.

>(Bedwa and Palasha stand facing each other for several moments before they begin.)

BEDWA

Give 'em the ol' frazzle dazzle, and I guess that really does explain most of it right there.

PALASHA

Time spent regretting not going to a lot of social events you really wanted to go to is officially fertile, rich manure.

BEDWA

(Joyful)

(pacing around while Palasha paces around in the other direction)

It's a biggie it's a biggie. Great! You've found a place. I like fertile ground because I like plants, I really turned a corner with plants walking around my neighborhood with Katherine and getting excited about plants that survive cold autumn air. Plants surround many people and animals and insects. The sun hits plants, changing their colors and shadows, every single day.

PALASHA

(Not sarcastic!)

Yeah that was hard, like real hard- wasn't it?

BEDWA

(Standing still on other side of stage)

It feels so vast, that I don't know if I can call it hard.

PALASHA

(Walking to him, standing a few feet apart facing each other)

Oh my gosh! I just realized who you might be!

BEDWA

And then the other thing wouldn't matter as much.

PALASHA

(Irritated)

No it would matter more!

BEDWA

It's so easy to...

PALASHA

Go into...

BEDWA

(Slowly start strolling side by side around stage, looking directly ahead)

Because it is decisive, because it's nostalgic, and because it's difficult.

PALASHA

Why are you so interested in difficult?

BEDWA

Maybe because easiness leads me where I often do not want to be! My hair both coily and curly today. I hadn't washed it for a while.

PALASHA

And you love that! Natural hair oil, you feel like it is getting an amazing product that your own scalp produces and provides and you don't even have to harvest it. Sometimes harder is better.

BEDWA

(Stopping, facing each other)

And you don't have to.

PALASHA

You kind of have to.

BEDWA

It's about that! It's about this!!

PALASHA

Once again in the course of your day almost every day, you make the discovery that things can stand for other things, very well. Really different things can really stand for something. 'Cause one thing we can agree on is meaning as important.

> (Both become very distracted, barely noticing each other, not really paying attention to what they are saying, but arranging many set pieces and "props" which had been off to the side, unnoticed. It is as though an invisible line separates each of their arrangements. They move them around, placing the "props" on set pieces.)

BEDWA

But you were still worried until very recently that it didn't work and you would somehow be obligated to report on that as very real.

PALASHA

I think I know what you're talking about—

BEDWA

Every time you shape words into a different language!!!

PALASHA

No really, it doesn't matter, we do that when we're babies.

BEDWA

How am I so less capable of certain confidences? Certain as in specific, not as in-

PALASHA

Certainly.

> (Continue arranging sets until a good stopping point is reached, and the two stand a few feet apart looking at each other).

BEDWA

How am I so less capable of certain confidences? Certain as in specific, not as in-

PALASHA

Certainly?

BEDWA

Ooo I just had a thought and it turned into a pictoral dream and then I forgot it immediately.

PALASHA

That's wonderful!

BEDWA

Are you upset?

PALASHA

Maybe, it just seems inordinately slow, like so slow, maybe too slow.

BEDWA

(Both face audience, not looking at each other)

Well maybe everything is! Or at least infinite things.

PALASHA

You're very comforting when you use the concept of the infinite.

BEDWA

Your friend showed up in ceremonial clothing, and you weren't sure if it was a good ritual or bad ritual.

PALASHA

(Pausing, thinking it over)

The clothes were white which I know seems a little too clean.

BEDWA

But what is clean but just a system of organization where dust particles, particles of soil, are placed in certain places.

PALASHA

You are interested in the assignment of things to things, aren't you?

BEDWA

In generalll..

PALASHA

You are lying!!

BEDWA

Was I kind of? Wait, hmm…

>(Taking each other's hands to form a sort of frame around their heads)

No, I mean, I don't think it's possible to lie about something so undefined, but I'm sure one could, anyway, it would seem really contradictory to lie about something really vague when all you're doing is thinking about things anyways.

PALASHA

There's a big difference between just thinking about things and talking about them.

> (At this point the two do a synchronized dance to a popular song; it should not be a love song so it doesn't imply they are grappling with being in love, even if they might be. Possible songs include Everything is Everything by Lauryn Hill, Celebration by Kool and The Gang)

BEDWA

> (The two finish their dance and face the audience)

Oh it seems like in this instance I am the responder, the rhythm of turn.

> (Face each other)

Oh good night.

PALASHA

Well OK!

> (They slap both of their hands to each others' hands four times, smile sincerely, then exit on opposite sides of the stage)

Shut the Front Door

by Tim Kabara

CHARACTERS

JIM RIVERA: is an 18 year old American male who listens to alternative rock. He is kinda sorta going out with Suzy Rosenberg.

SUZY ROSENBERG: is an 18 year old American female who listens to alternative rock. She is kinda sorta going out with Jim Rivera. They met at a local alternative rock festival, the WFSTIVAL, just a few weeks ago.

MAN FROM FUTURE: is, seemingly, a man from the future who has come to warn of great dangers. He is older and bears a passing resemblance to JIM RIVERA.

SETTING

Funk's Democratic Coffee Spot in the Baltimore neighborhood of Fell's Point. It was often frequented by 1990s alternative types.

ACT I

SCENE 1

We are in the above-mentioned coffee shop in the late spring/ early summer of 1994. Music is playing which indicates this. The lighting is "normal". There is a table and two chairs. Seated in the two chairs are JIM RIVERA and SUZY ROSENBERG. Both are drinking coffee, often taking sips while the other one speaks. Both are dressed as Alternative Rock enthusiasts would be in the late spring/ early summer of 1994, tempered by the dress code they had grown accustomed to in private single-gender Catholic school. They have just both been recently liberated from these constrictions via graduation. They have been talking for some time, but the music drops down and we can now hear what they are saying.

JIM RIVERA

... but I mean if your parents say that you can't go for a real reason, then that's one thing, but the whole car thing is, like, totally technical.

SUZY ROSENBERG

Yeah. They're just worried about me.

JIM RIVERA

Yeah. Well if you can go, do you think it would be cool if I stayed with you guys?

SUZY ROSENBERG

I don't know... the rental company seems pretty strict about it being all girls..

JIM RIVERA

(defeated)

Yeah...

SUZY ROSENBERG

(shyly, but flirtatiously)

But, you know, we could probably sneak you in or something.

JIM RIVERA

(clearly excited about this)

Yeah! That would be awesome! Like an 80s movie! I can see it on the marquee: "Spring Break '94"!

SUZY ROSENBERG

(laughing, amused)

Yeah! You might have to dress up in drag, you know.

JIM RIVERA

(confidently)

Oh, I can do drag! That's not an issue.

(leans in conspiratorially, looks around)

And, by then, I should have gotten some good acid, and then maybe we -

SUZY ROSENBERG

(caught off guard)

Acid?

JIM RIVERA

You know, LSD?

SUZY ROSENBERG

(miffed)

I know what acid is.

JIM RIVERA

Well, anyway, I have this friend, right, and he has recently been getting fairly speedy low grade stuff, but by then he should have gotten some primo stuff... Jesus Christ! And then, well, we could-

SUZY ROSENBERG

Jesus Christ?

JIM RIVERA

Yeah! This stuff, Jesus Christ, they say is really pure, really good. Anyway, I really think we should take acid together sometime.

SUZY ROSENBERG

> (startled but trying to appear cool with this proposal)

Yeah! Um... I'm gonna get some more coffee, okay?

JIM RIVERA

Okay!

> (SUZY exits the stage. Jim stares after her longingly, oblivious to her hesitation.)

> (The 1994 music that has been playing in the background slows down and stops, like when you stop a direct drive turntable from rotating. There is a lighting change to accompany the music change. The lighting is now "weird.")

> (MAN FROM FUTURE stumbles onto the stage, clutching some sort of metallic device with

switches and knobs. The device resembles something you would use to control remote-control cars or airplanes. He is dressed in a white lab coat which has powder burns on it and is dressed otherwise in a manner appropriate for the early part of the second decade of the Twenty-First century. He looks around in wonderment.)

MAN FROM FUTURE

Holy snit! It worked!

(turns to Jim)

Hey! Hi! Hello!

JIM RIVERA

Um... hey, man.

MAN FROM FUTURE

Yeah! Wow! Hi! Um... listen up, okay? I don't have a lot of time. I'm here from the future.

JIM RIVERA

What?

MAN FROM FUTURE

Long story. Can I sit down?

Jim Rivera gestures tentatively for the man to sit and he does so in Suzy's chair.

JIM RIVERA

Look, man... I don't have any change. And you're not supposed to bother the patrons, okay?

(starts looking around)

Woah... wait a minute. How come everything's slowing down?

MAN FROM FUTURE

(matter-of-factly)

Because the device does that. But that doesn't matter now! I have just a few minutes here to tell you important things.

(self-importantly)

I come with a message from the future!

JIM RIVERA

Man, duck the future!

(puzzled)

Why the duck did I just say "duck" when I meant to say -

MAN FROM FUTURE

(a little embarrassed)

Uh... yeah. The device does that also. We can't figure out why. Anyway-

JIM RIVERA

(tuning in again to his surroundings)

Holy snit, man! Everybody here is, like, frozen!

(fearfully)

Man, I gotta stop doing acid! Gooch told me to take it easy, but did I listen, no I didn't! Duck, man! Motherducking snit!

MAN FROM FUTURE

(placating)

Calm down. Everything is okay. You're going to be fine.

JIM RIVERA

(sharply)

How would you know?

MAN FROM FUTURE

I know because I'm you. In the future.

JIM RIVERA

You're me?

MAN FROM FUTURE

(a bit sanctimoniously)

Yes, Jim. Yes, I am. I am you in the future.

JIM RIVERA

(incredulous)

No way! I got old, man! You're totally old!

MAN FROM FUTURE

(aware of this sad fact)

Yeah, I know. Now, listen up!

(pedantically, in the manner of a college professor)

There are many important things you need to know about the future. First of all, the environment. There is a lot that you can do in 1994 to help offset-

JIM RIVERA

- wait wait. What about virtual sex?

MAN FROM FUTURE

Huh?

JIM RIVERA

(kind of a little embarrassed)

I got this magazine at Reptilian Records and it's called Future Sex, right? And, like, in that magazine it says that in the future people can have virtual sex, like, for real!

MAN FROM FUTURE

(remembering, with a touch of fondness)

Ah yes... I remember those magazines.

JIM RIVERA

Yeah, man. Pretty cool stuff...

MAN FROM FUTURE

Yeah...

(snaps out of his reverie)

But anyway, that's not important! What's important is that the environment is in a lot of trouble and we need to-

JIM RIVERA

Woah! Hold on, old man! Not important? That's totally important! Virtual sex?

MAN FROM FUTURE

Look, I understand that right now you are a teenager and a virgin-

JIM RIVERA

(defensively)

Shut up!

MAN FROM FUTURE

I know you are lying to people about that. Remember, I'm you?

JIM RIVERA

(accepting this but still stung)

Oh yeah... right.

MAN FROM FUTURE

So...

(looks at the device which is counting down the time)

okay. Forget the environment. Virtual sex? I'll tell you all about that! There is this thing called the Internet, right? Right?

(assumes JIM knows about this thing)

JIM RIVERA

(has never heard of this thing)

Um... okay.

MAN FROM FUTURE

And it is going to make large parts of life easier.

JIM RIVERA

Sounds good...

MAN FROM FUTURE

Well, yes... but is is also going to cause lots of problems. Big problems!

(struggling)

It is a series of ... connected computers talking... uh...

JIM RIVERA

(lightbulb goes off)

Wait, you mean that thing like the BBS chat thing or whatever?

MAN FROM FUTURE

Yes! That's it!

JIM RIVERA

Dude, that thing sucks! It ties up your phone line and it's for nerds!

MAN FROM FUTURE

Well, okay. but-

JIM RIVERA

I'm not a nerd, man. Next!

MAN FROM FUTURE

But you don't understand-

JIM RIVERA

I do understand! Internet! Got it. Whatever. Next!

MAN FROM FUTURE

(clearly frustrated by JIM's adolescent impudence)

Oh man... I should have written some more of these things down!

(pulls out a piece of paper, examines it)

A-ha! Yes, you may not care about the Internet, Jim, but I have yet to tell you of... the Facebook.

JIM RIVERA

Okay, fine. What's the Facebook?

An abridged version of the more dramatic and recognizable parts of the theme from the film Terminator, "The Terminator" begins to play in the background.

MAN FROM FUTURE

What we did not know in your time was that the Internet was watching us, taking our data as we gave it freely, learning about us so that it could one day... enslave us.

JIM RIVERA

Man... that sucks. What can I do about it?

MAN FROM FUTURE

hand over the piece of paper, which JIM RIVERA glances at.

MAN FROM FUTURE

> (growing increasingly frenzied and impassioned, eventually rising from his seat)

You must eliminate the people on this list! They were the architects of the Facebook! They are the causers of humanity's downfall! In the future Jim, all anyone does is check this insidious device, enslaved by hand-held machines! You want to hang out and they spend the entire evening staring at their hand! You know not of this, Jim, and I want you to never know of it! You must help us fight the future! I didn't want to scare you, but... my time grows short!

The music reaches a crescendo and then stops shortly after the end of the this outburst. MAN FROM FUTURE fall back into his seat, surprised at his emotional outburst.

JIM RIVERA

Dramatic much? Look, you want me to kill some people, right? Duck that. I don't believe in solving problems through violence, man.

(a little haughtily)

I'm a pacifist.

MAN FROM FUTURE

(wearily, remembering)

Oh yeah... I forgot. You took that punch over a girl...

JIM RIVERA

(clearly takes pride in this)

Yes, I am a man of principle! I did not punch back. I turned the other cheek!

MAN FROM FUTURE

(with the sad wisdom of age and experience)

You know she slept with that guy eventually, after you turned the other cheek...

JIM RIVERA

What? No! No way! I mean we don't talk much anymore but-

MAN FROM FUTURE

Let me pull back here for a sec. I do have some good news.

JIM RIVERA

Okay. Shoot.

MAN FROM FUTURE

The girl you are on a date with?

Bem's Hypothesis

by Erin Gleeson

CHARACTERS

ROGER: Vaguely unkempt, but not ridiculously so. He just gives off the impression that he typically takes the easy way out. Wears glasses.

TEDDY: Semi-focused, goal oriented. A moderate wienie, but you can kind of understand where she's coming from.

PUPPET ROGER: Roger as a little kid. Also wears glasses. Glockenspiel player: This could be Teddy, but if she doesn't know how it could be anyone else that can play it.

SCENE ONE

(Lights up on ROGER sitting at a table surrounded by books. He's reading from one and taking notes. Onstage, there are miscellaneous items strewn about: an inflated balloon, an open umbrella, a boot, etc. TEDDY enters with a bag full of stuff.)

TEDDY

Okay, here's everything you asked for.

ROGER

Perfect.

TEDDY

> (looking around at all the stuff onstage, stepping over something)

So how have you been doing?

ROGER

Very well, thank you. I read this article about a well-respected scientist. He discovered that studying after a test can actually improve your grade.

TEDDY

Get out of here.

ROGER

It's true. People like this guy and everything, so it's definitely not bullshit.

TEDDY

And what, you want to do better in high school now?

ROGER

Not exactly. What if my life is only as good as it is because I'm working on it now?

> (suddenly terrified, gripping the books)

What if this is the only thing keeping me afloat?

TEDDY

You're fine.

ROGER

Maybe this guy is right, though. Maybe we can send our thoughts and intentions back in time.

TEDDY

(looking into the bag she's holding)

So you had me drive over here with my rollerskates and pinwheels so your brain could time travel?

ROGER

I only need one rollerskate, but yes. When I was a kid, I spent weeks working on this Rube Goldberg device. I wanted to set up all of this stuff

(waves a hand toward the items strewn about)

and rig it so that it would turn off my bedroom light before bed.

TEDDY

Did you figure it out?

ROGER

No. But maybe now I can figure it out, send those brainwaves back in time and give myself the life I always wanted.

TEDDY

A life where it takes you five minutes to turn out the light.

ROGER

(shrugs)

Maybe if I figured it out, it would have boosted my self-confidence.

TEDDY

Well, I'll leave you to it. Hey, me and Lenny are going to the movies tonight. Wanna come?

ROGER

(Turning back to his book, head in hand. His cheek is smushed against his palm.)

I can't; I've got this geometry test twelve years ago.

(Black out.)

SCENE TWO

(A folded newspaper on a black back- ground spins. You know, like in old movies. You should also play a sound clip of that music they usually play over such things. Am I making sense? The paper slows to a stop and we see that it reads:

HEADLINE: "Grown man passes Geometry test."

SUBHEADLINE: "I don't know who let him take it," said teacher.

You could also do this with video if the text is too hard to read, though I would prefer that it be a real prop onstage.)

SCENE THREE

(Lights up on TEDDY jogging, stage right. It would be great to have a background on rollers, so that it looks like she's really moving.)

> (Lights up on ROGER, stage left. He's holding a list)
>
> (The two are obviously in different locations.)

ROGER

> (Glancing at the list. It looks like he's remembering each incident as he goes through it.)

I'm sorry. I didn't realize I shouldn't use your computer for porn. I didn't know I left it on the desktop, and I definitely didn't know your mom would come over and need to use MapQuest.

I'm sorry I forgot to feed your cat while you were away; I'm glad he didn't die.

I'm sorry.

I'm sorry.

I'm very sorry.

> (TEDDY stops and pulls out a cell phone. She dials a number. ROGER's phone rings. He picks it up. It's an old fashioned phone, with a coiled cord and everything. This could be real or it could be a cutout.)

ROGER

Hello?

TEDDY

Hey, it's Teddy. Are you busy?

ROGER

No, I was just sending things I should have said back in time.

TEDDY

(unphased by this)

I think you might be sort of right about the brainwaves thing.

ROGER

Yeah, I passed the shit out of that geometry test.

TEDDY

Well yeah, but I just had my own experience. I was just jogging and remembering this race I lost when I was ten. And so I'm running and pushing myself, and then all of a sudden, I feel a sense of accomplishment about that race. Like my training now helped me to do better then.

ROGER

See, I knew you'd be a believer! This morning, I figured out the Rube Goldberg thing too.

TEDDY

You were able to turn the light out?

ROGER

Yeah!

(Teddy is thrilled.)

Now that you understand where I'm coming from, I need your help with another childhood dream of mine.

(Black out.)

SCENE FOUR

(Lights up on ROGER in a white jumpsuit and a cardboard space helmet. He's on a red surface and

> holding a flag with a picture of his own face on it. Nearby, there's a cardboard cutout of a space shuttle. TEDDY sits at a desk wearing a white shirt, headset and tie and smoking a cigarette, á la NASA mission control circa 1969.)

(TEDDY ashes into an ash tray.)

TEDDY

MacArthur, do you copy?

ROGER

Copy that, Houston.

> (He places the flag on the surface. He moves as if gravity is much different where he is. He ambles over to the shuttle and pretends to drive it back to Earth. He stops next to TEDDY, gripping the shuttle in both hands. He knocks the helmet off his head with one hand.)

ROGER

You think it worked?

TEDDY

(disappointed)

I think we'd need to know a lot more about engineering for Past You to be able to make it to Mars.

ROGER

I thought that might be a problem. Maybe I should hit the books some more. I mean, if I figured out the Rube Goldberg thing and that Geometry test, Mars can't be all that hard, right? (A beat.) Hey, wait a minute. I've got a feeling coming on.

TEDDY

Oh yeah? What's up?

ROGER

(thoughtfully)

Well. It feels like everything's fine. Like I'm a capable person. I feel like I have faith in my own abilities.

TEDDY

Hmm. What do you think Past You is up to?

(Roger shrugs.)

(Black out.)

SCENE FIVE

(Lights up on a puppet stage. It should be obvious that this is the past. Everything could be in greyscale like an old movie or something like that. PUPPET ROGER is lying in bed and his room is full of his Rube Goldberg device.)

(TEDDY or SOMEONE is playing the glockenspiel in the background.

(PUPPET ROGER pushes a rollerskate down a ramp, setting off a series of events. PUPPET ROGER claps in delight. The objects do just what he wanted: they successfully click off the light switch.)

(Black out.)

Packing/Pecking

A short play of words and movement

by Juanita Rockwell

CHARACTERS
CECE: A quiet woman

JAY: Cece's brother, a quiet man

JOHNNY: Cece's recent ex

CHRISTINE: Jay's recent ex

SETTING
An empty space littered with sunflower seeds.

HINT
Most lines are best delivered directly to the audience.

Don't feel restrained to the exclusive use of realistic movements, if you're good at that sort of thing. However, the piece can work well performed very simply, just by letting the language be the movement. Lots of yarn and feathers will help.

And the line divisions are there to help with finding the rhythm – punctuation is key.

>(CECE and JAY enter from opposite sides of the stage, each bringing out a steamer trunk, setting it deliberately in place and opening the lid.)
>
>(They each peer inside their respective trunks, briefly, then exit whence they came.)

> (CHRISTINE and JOHNNY enter, Johnny crossing to Cece's trunk, and Christine crossing to Jay's trunk, each with pen and paper in hand. They investigate the contents of their respective trunks, taking notes, and exit.)
>
> (Christine and Johnny return, begin picking up sunflower seeds off the ground and eating them.)

CHRISTINE

First, I said
Nobody's going anywhere until we get all this down in writing.

JOHNNY

For one thing.
It was a seriously inconvenient time for Cece to get that surgery.
She gets home.
Commandeers the bedroom with all that paraphernalia from the hospital.
And then she's got to drag her mother into my life?

> (to Christine)

You know what a pain their mother is.

> (Johnny pauses to spit out a sunflower seed.)

So I've got those two in my hair every day.
Her mom clucking over her and that stupid oxygen tent like she's some sort of invalid.
The old lady shrinks the sleeves on one of my shirts
Lets the weeds practically take over the lawn
Only cleans Ariadne's shitbox once a day so it reeks like hell.
The house isn't even as clean as Cece kept it.
Certainly not to my standards.

And she uses weird spices in her cooking.
I didn't let Cece put that weird crap in my food but did you ever try to stand between her mom and the spice rack?

>(Cece enters with an armful of spice jars and Jay enters with a folded paisley shawl. They each put the items in their separate trunks and exit.)

CHRISTINE

As if I didn't know he already took that big paisley shawl
I mean it wasn't in my colors
I'm a winter
But I saw one like it on the Sotheby's website that started bidding at $3,500.
Started!

JOHNNY

I need my mornings. I told her that on our first date.
Absolute quiet before noon.
She learned. Eventually.
But her mother? Absolutely impossible.
Pots and pans rattling. The vacuum blaring. The laundry going.
I could barely concentrate on my game with all the racket.

CHRISTINE

The old lady has ALWAYS been impossible but the crying and carrying on about how the shawl had to "stay in the family?"
I mean crazy bitch gave it to the two of us.
She conveniently forgets that Jay and I were already sort of together then, I mean Tad and I were pretty much separated, well I was GOING to tell Tad I was leaving him and I was only at his place about half the time by that time, so I might as well have been living with Jay when his mom gave him the damn shawl and that would make us almost common law in some states so

it's like community property, right?
And it's not like it cost HER anything.
And now Jay wants Cece to have it?

JOHNNY

Cece refused to cook the whole time her mother was there.
Even though she knew I hated the old bag's cooking.
Too dangerous?
Come on, her oxygen had a special monitor for leaks.
"Dangerous."
What a wuss.
As long as she didn't put the damn tank in the oven it was plenty safe.
She just didn't want to cook.

>   (Christine carefully spits a
>   sunflower shell into a tissue
>   before speaking.)

CHRISTINE

I'm definitely keeping the alabaster vase.
Old as DIRT, cost a fortune, had to clean out the account to buy it
But whatever, it's an investment
Worth ten times what I paid for it on Ebay.
Got it from a vet - hey, support the troops, right?
Guy says he, uh, "liberated" it from some joint in Baghdad, says it was just crammed in a corner of some old building piled to the rafters with stuff
Three thousand, four thousand years old
They won't miss it
They're CRAWLING with that shit over there.
Scratch any patch of sand and there's some priceless piece of crap.
Hey, "to the victor..." right?

JOHNNY

They were so in on it together, we should have known.
"The Brother-Sister Bond."
You and I, Christine, we were the outsiders.
How can a mere lover compete with blood?
They had some secret code.
Never finished a sentence when the other one was there.
Like some sort of alien life form psychically connected through Pod-Mind.
Their own silent language.

CHRISTINE

Furtive looks.

JOHNNY

"Chance" meetings.

CHRISTINE

Occult rituals.

JOHNNY

They always had some top secret complicated project going on.
Their heads together, hands like little spiders always hooking one thing to another.
Then sooner or later, you, all unsuspecting, end up walking into it and suddenly it's in your hair all sticky and...
I don't know.

CHRISTINE

I know, right?
He drifts away from you in the middle of a conversation
It's like gravity isn't the same for him
I mean my feet are on the GROUND

But Jay, little wisps of cloud float in and out of his ears when
you're trying to talk to him.

> (Cece enters again with a picture
> frame wrapped in cloth, places it
> lovingly in her trunk, and exits.)

JOHNNY

So the stitches finally heal and she's finally out of bed.
And her mom leaves. Finally.
So I try to spruce things up a little
And Cece goes Psycho for real.
Just some dusty self-portrait by her great-grandmother.
Supposed to be such a big whooptidoodle deal.
It looked so much better after I touched it up.
I bet great-grandma would have thanked me.
A little skillful shading around her cheeks and eyes and
BAM! she looks like a fashion model and not some starving artist
in a backward village somewhere.
I mean if her paintings were really any good
Wouldn't she have taken more of them with her when she
escaped?

> (Jay enters with some antique
> carved paint rollers, puts them
> carefully in his trunk and exits.)

CHRISTINE

He said he doesn't even want to look at the vase
Makes him "uncomfortable"
Doesn't even want me to take it out of the box until he's moved
out.
It's alabaster for chrissake, worth as much as my Porsche
And he's worrying about PROVENANCE?
Fine with me.
His idea of a treasure is some grungy old paint rollers he got in a

flea market in Warsaw
(Not even one of the pretty cities)
Had these kitschy carved patterns on them for rolled borders along the ceiling
Something that belongs in a stuffy doily-covered parlor somewhere.
I'm all for wall treatments, but more like some elegant Ralph Lauren sueded effect on a dining room wall.
I mean DWELL is my bible, but come on, not this shit.
Those rolls were all fucked up, too
One had a bullet-hole in it for chrissake.

> (During the next segment, Cece enters again, holding the end of a very long piece of red yarn that trails offstage. She keeps pulling at the yarn, endlessly, rolling it into a ball that gets bigger and bigger and bigger as she pulls more and more yarn from offstage, throughout the scene.)

JOHNNY

After the portrait incident she just folds up on me.
Moves to some little planet in her head.
And she's not doing jack shit around the house, right?
Except knitting.
Every day.
Every night.

> (As Cece continues to pull red yarn onto the stage, Jay enters with a beautiful wabi-sabi Japanese tea bowl, carefully folds an elegant silk napkin, and puts them both in the trunk.)

CHRISTINE

"Irreconcilable differences" isn't that what they call it?
What was I thinking, should have known from our first date
Invites me in for TEA
Weird enough right there
And it's not just tea, it's a freakin' production.

JOHNNY

She starts out saying it's a sock.
Then she's saying scarf. Then it's a shawl. A cape.
But she's still knitting.
And it's getting huge:
An afghan for the TV couch. A blanket.
And I say that thing's getting too big for our California King
Let alone a normal bed.
And then she says she's knitting a tent.
For camping.
And I'm like, what?

CHRISTINE

I mean really
What kind of man gets THAT involved in a stupid cup of tea?
Totally gay, that fussy little bamboo whisk and some napkin
that's so freakin' SPECIAL he's all upset when I use it to cover up
Cecilia's puke until he can come home and clean it up.
Well she's HIS cat.
And you know that bamboo thing could hold all kinds of germs:
Staph, strep, influenza, E.coli, salmonella, smallpox, genital
herpes, UTI's, TB, enterococcus, HIV, Ebola, hemorrhagic fever
You name it.
And those bowls are freakin' ugly, some of them even look
I don't know,
Bent.

JOHNNY

Finally says it's a "house cozy."
What the fuck.
Said she wanted to make a tea cozy, but for the whole fucking house.
Total wacko.
And then her mom acts like knitting a fucking "house cozy" isn't certifiable.

CECE

(looking up from her yarn)

I want everything in the house to be cozy, not just the tea pot.

JOHNNY

Total nutjob.

CHRISTINE

A cup of tea, FINE, so nuke a cup of Lipton's and get on with your day.

JOHNNY

I had to get out of there.
At least for a couple of hours until dinner's ready.

CHRISTINE

And then there were the ducks.

JOHNNY

So I storm out the front door, jump in the Hummer and take off.

CHRISTINE

He was raising those filthy birds in our backyard
Wanted them for the feathers

He'd gather them up every day and stuff them in everything:
Pillows, quilts, vests, slippers, you name it.

JOHNNY

The traffic was miserable in town so I just headed out
For wherever.
Driving and driving and driving...

CHRISTINE

It took him weeks to get enough feathers to do much of anything
at all so I said he should just pluck the fuckers but NOOO
Said they were some weird kind of Icelandic duck that pluck out
their own damn feathers.
Well they certainly took their sweet time about it.
And the noise:
Quack quack quack quack quack quack quack quack quack...
Plucking my last nerve.

>   (Jay finds a feather on his shirt,
>   puts it in his palm, blows it into
>   the air, watches it drift.)

JAY

That's just how they sing.
Everything has a song.
And that's how they sing.

CHRISTINE

Quack quack quack quack quack quack quack quack quack quack
quack quack quack...

JOHNNY

And driving and driving.
Looking for a sign.
I was halfway around the beltway when I finally saw one.

In flashing neon, just off the exit.
Decided to stop in for a little libation and feminine entertainment.

> (Jay sings an odd but lovely little tune, almost to himself, as Cece pulls more yarn from offstage.)

CHRISTINE

They eventually stopped quacking so much but the way Jay got them to clam up was even more disturbing.
Creepy, really.
He'd be wandering around the back end of the yard going from nest to nest
Singing
Picking through each ratty stack of straw for those TINY little feathers, putting them one by one in a bag like they were spun out of gold
Those stupid ducks waddling along after him, staring at him silently.
He'd sit on a rock with a bag full of down and sing to them
Nestled in at his feet like puppies.
Or feathered rats.
The Pied Piper of Duckville.

> (Jay starts pulling downy feathers out of his pockets and out of the trunk, letting the tiny things drift and pile around his feet, as Cece continues to pull more red yarn from offstage.)

JOHNNY

How was I supposed to know that her damn yarn was caught on my belt buckle?
I'd already pulled into the lot at Wet n' Wild.

Hopped out of the Hummer, a roll of twenties in my pocket
Ready for the nearest G-string.
But when I got out and turned back around to lock the door
My feet were a tangle of red.
I thought I was bleeding.
That thin red line trickling down my legs
Wrapped around my ankles
Winding out across the parking lot
Between the rows of Jeeps and trucks
Stretching out as far as I could see.
Must have gone all the way through the city and around the damn beltway.

> (Johnny is tangled in red yarn and Christine is plagued by feathers.)

CHRISTINE

But it was those fucking feathers that finally put me over the edge.
Jay said they have these teeny sort of tiny hooks in them
Makes them cling together
Supposed to make them warmer but it really just makes them more annoying.
They were everywhere, stuck to everything
I'd find them in bed
Stuck to my cashmere sweaters
Stuck in my HAIR.
I thought I was turning gray
It was those damn feathers.

> (Feathers are everywhere, sticking to the giant ball of red yarn, to Cece, to Jay . The two of them play in the swirl of feathers like snow.)

JOHNNY

Late that night when I got home
Drunk as a bicycle
All that was left was a little tug of red yarn
Disappearing down the driveway.

CHRISTINE

So I started making this list
I've got it all down and he's not getting another damn thing.
Except those feathers.
He can have those.

> (Johnny spits out a sunflower seed.)

JOHNNY

Just a sad little squiggle of red.

> (Jay and Cece's snow-dance of feathers and yarn continues until the lights dim.)

Snowverdose

A play in one act

by Tom Foran

CHARACTERS

JACK: a guy, could be anywhere from college-aged to early middle-aged, edgy, tends to go to extremes.

MIKE: a guy, roughly the same age as Jack, (seemingly) more relaxed and optimistic.

VOICE OFFSTAGE: preferably female, young, pragmatic

*note: JACK and MIKE could easily be made female characters by necessity or by choice, but I think the sudden shift to violence suits a male psyche a bit better.

SETTING

There are various small tables around the stage, ideally around six or so, each with a different complex board game, things involving many small pieces and patience (Chess, RISK, Go, Monopoly, etc). JACK and MIKE sit at a table, playing RISK. They are totally involved in the game and concentrate deeply. They both look a little dirty, as though they have not been outside in a few days. The stage is lit by cordless lights, like kerosene or battery-operated lamps. The entire script should be thought of as more like an outline than an actual set in stone "scene." As long as the performers get the gist across, they need not worry about every single line being perfect. The scene also assumes an at least rudimentary knowledge of classic board games on the part of the actors, director, and audience.

JACK

(looking at the board, not looking up at MIKE)

I'm attacking Kamchatka from Irkutsk.

MIKE

(also not looking up)

With how many?

JACK

Three.

MIKE

Okay.

(they roll their respective dice, look at them, look at the board, and silently move their respective pieces around)

MIKE

I'm attacking Quebec from Greenland.

JACK

With how many?

MIKE

Four.

JACK

Okay.

(they repeat the above actions. JACK then looks up at MIKE for the first time, sighs, leans back in his chair.)

MIKE

What?

JACK

Wanna switch?

MIKE

(finally looking up)

Right now?

JACK

Yeah.

MIKE

Okay, sure.

(very carefully, so as not to disturb any of the pieces, they slide the table off to one side and slide another into its place, also painfully carefully. On this table is a chessboard, midgame. They silently study the game for a few moments, until JACK moves a piece, hits a chess clock timer.)

JACK

Check.

(another moment of silent study, then MIKE moves a piece, hits the chess clock timer. Another moment of silent study, then JACK moves a piece, hits the chess clock timer. Another moment of silent study, then MIKE moves a piece, hits the chess clock timer. Another moment of silent study, then JACK

> leans back in his chair and looks up, sighs
> again.)

MIKE

Bored of this now too?

JACK

Yeah.

MIKE

Wanna switch?

JACK

Okay, sure.

> (very carefully, as before, they shift the table to
> now switch it out for a table with a backgammon
> set on it. They silently study the game, as before.
> JACK lifts his hand, as if about to grab the dice
> and make a move, then lets it fall back down,
> discouraged.)

JACK

I don't even fucking like backgammon.

MIKE

What?

JACK

I hate backgammon. My brother used to make me play with him when we were little and he was better than me and the rule was whenever someone lost the winner got to throw all the pieces at the back of the loser's head. It was his stupid rule he made up because he was good at backgammon and I sucked at it and he always beat me and it was just an excuse for him to throw shit at my head.

> (JACK stares off, despondent, MIKE looks around awkwardly.)

MIKE

Okay, so I guess we can be done with backgammon for now.

> (He shifts the table as before and is about to shift in another with a game of Battleship set up on it when JACK interrupts him.)

JACK

Oh, what's the point? We're gonna die.

MIKE

Knock it off.

JACK

When was the last time you saw the sun?

MIKE

Like... what day is it?

JACK

Thursday.

MIKE

Like Saturday.

JACK

How can you be so casual about that? That's a big deal!

MIKE

Could be worse.

JACK

(becoming more agitated, eventually flailing his arms around like a lunatic)

Your optimism is killing me. We can't even see out the windows, there's so much snow! No electricity, no TV, no Internet, the radio's dead, the heat's going! We are entombed! WE HAVE BECOME CORPSES!

MIKE

Imagine what people did four hundred years ago! Or like the explorers to the South Pole. They probably had it way worse.

JACK

(as if not hearing him)

We have no means of contact with the outside world. None whatsoever. It might still be snowing right now. It might keep snowing for another week. This could be the Snowpocalypse.

MIKE

The what?

JACK

The Snowmaggedon, man! Ragnarok is upon us! This is the fimbulwinter! Giant wolves have eaten the sun! The dead shall rise!

MIKE

Don't you think you're overreacting?

(beat. JACK stares)

JACK

Overreacting? OVERREACTING? We're gonna run out of food soon, you moron!

MIKE

Then we'll hibernate.

JACK

(this is the stupidest thing he's ever heard)

Hibernate? What are you, a bear?

MIKE

Yeah, why not? Hibernate, man. You go into a sleep-state, kind of like a coma, living off of your body's fat reserves until you can go outside again.

JACK

No, Michael, that's starvation. Your brain starts to hallucinate all kindsa crazy things, like I'll look at you and your head will turn into a turkey sandwich and you'll look at me and see lasagna like in a friggin' Daffy Duck cartoon and we'll be crazed and try to eat each other and then in three months when they dig us out I'll have gone feral and I'll be sitting in a corner, trying to suck the marrow out of your bones. Like that soccer team in the mountains when their plane crashed.

MIKE

Rugby.

JACK

What?

MIKE

It was a rugby team, I think.

JACK

No it wasn't, they made a movie about it, I remember.

MIKE

Oh.

(beat.)

What makes you think you'd win, anyway?

(JACK guffaws loudly)

MIKE

Whatever. I don't think it will be like that at all. Our ancestors, man, they had it way worse than us. Like the cavemen, they had the ice age and shit. They were in a pretty similar situation to us, right? Hunkered down, in a cave, it's dark, they're bored, maybe a little paranoid (JACK looks at him sharply), SOOOO they try to keep their minds off of it! They paint the walls—

JACK

(overlapping under his breath)

I'll paint the walls with your blood.

MIKE

—they start to invent language and religion and stuff, and, wait, what?

JACK

Oh, nothing! Do go on with your inane fantasy, Michael. I'm sure your delusion will pass the time better than fucking backgammon.

MIKE

Hey, man, no need to be a jerk about it. I'm stuck here too!

JACK

(getting worked up again)

Michael, those were cavemen; their idea of technology was a sharpened stick. They were just really tall chimps, alright? Don't compare us to them; they didn't even know to wipe their asses so they were barely more than animals. They were not men like us. We have been drenched in technology. We're saturated in the garbage, we're the ADD generation, man, look at us, we can't even focus on one goddamn board game for more than twenty seconds! WE CANNOT LIVE LIKE THIS!

MIKE

Okay, maybe somebody might need a nap...

JACK

FUCK you.

(beat)

MIKE

(reaching into his pocket, pulling out a cribbage set)

How about we—

JACK

DON'T YOU DARE. If you value your life at all, do not start another game.

MIKE

Hey, they pass the time, right? Besides, they're all we've got. If we can just focus on the games, we can—

(JACK wordlessly and nonchalantly flips the nearest game off its table, throwing pieces everywhere)

MIKE

WHAT ARE YOU DOING?!?!

JACK

Enough of this shit.

MIKE

(frantically trying to gather the pieces)

What have you done?

Why would you do that?

JACK

I'm setting us free, Mikey. Let's take control of our fates!

MIKE

(sitting on the floor, on the verge of tears, with board game pieces falling from between his fingers)

That wasn't Candyland, Jack! That was Monopoly (or whatever it happened to be)! We'd been playing for THREE DAYS!

JACK

Screw it.

MIKE

"Screw it?"

JACK

Screw 'em all.

> (He knocks over a couple more games, pieces go flying into the audience, MIKE rocks back and forth on the ground. JACK surveys what he's done, somewhat satisfied, then he sees RISK, the big one, the final one)

And you, you god-awful rotten bastard.

MIKE

DON'T TOUCH THAT!!!

JACK

> (With his hand on the edge of the table)

I'm gonna set you free, Michael...

MIKE

I swear by all that is holy, if you mess around with the RISK board I will do something so terrible my brain cannot even think of it yet.

JACK

Sounds like exactly what we need!

MIKE

> (desperate)

Jack, please, be reasonable here, now...

JACK

No, no, no, it was REASON got us into this mess! Reason was us saying, "we can't go outside, let's bust out the old board games, it'll be FUN." We need to get a little NUTS!

MIKE

I'm begging you, Jack, please, if you value our friendship at all—

JACK

It's because of how much I love you that I gotta do this. It's tough love, man, because this is a crutch that is preventing you from running free like the gazelle, or whatever you are! You're a junkie and I'm about to make you go cold turkey.

MIKE

Don't you—

>(JACK flips the game, pieces scatter everywhere, MIKE finally looses it)

MIKE

-oh no you monster you fucking MONSTER!!!

>(He leaps up, wrestles JACK to the ground, begins to strangle him)

FUCK YOU FUCK YOU FUCK YOU!!! FUCK YOUR FAVORITE COLOR, FUCK EVERYTHING YOU EVER LOVED, FUCK YOUR UNBORN CHILDREN, FUCK YOUR HOPES AND DREAMS, FUCK YOUR FAVORITE DEAD RELATIVE, FUCK YOUR CHILDHOOD PETS—

>(JACK stabs him in the side of the head with a chess piece, something nice and sharp)

AAAUGH!

>(JACK coughs and clutches at his throat, rubbing his neck for a few moments while MIKE moans and whines, clutching his head. Things quiet down for a second or two as the pain subsides.)

JACK

(gasping)

Oh, but don't you feel better, Mikey, now that you're a real caveman again?!

                MIKE

A little.

      (beat)

             BUT STILL FUCK YOU JACK

      (he lunges at JACK again, but JACK evades him. MIKE crashes into the pieces, RISK men in his hair, laying on the ground, spent, perhaps weeping, maybe a little blood trickles down the side of his face. JACK springs to his feet)

                JACK

I like the way I'm feeling, Michael! I feel like my eyes have been opened. I feel like I'm waking up after sleeping for a thousand years! I CAN SEE FOREVER!

                MIKE

      (whispered softly)

I hate you.

                JACK

      (barely listening, getting hyped up again)

No you don't. I'm setting us free. We're doomed in our little cave, Michael, but if we take charge! Control our own fate! Show the cruel, remorseless, abandoning god above us that he can't fire us, because we quit!

      (he looks up, shakes his fist)

I'VE DECLARED WAR ON MY BODY! Ha ha ha!

>   (he grabs MIKE, rolls him over onto his back,
>   and holds his face, almost like a father)

You will not freeze, you will not starve, you will not go mad. No, Michael, none of these fates are fitting for one such as you. YOU WILL PERISH IN FLAMES. In FLAMES, Michael! Like the glorious Vikings of old, destined for Valhalla, on a boat in a frozen lake piled high with their treasures, a monument of fire! GODS will bow before us, Michael!

>   (he exits, laughing like a nutcase, MIKE curls
>   into a fetal position amidst the pieces on the
>   floor, maybe he begins to suck his thumb)

>   MIKE
>
>   (crying and muttering to himself
>   existentially)

Why did he have to ruin RISK? Why RISK? I could understand the others. But why RISK? That was all I had...

>   (JACK runs back in, holding a gallon of milk and
>   a bottle of Tequila. He takes a disturbingly large
>   glug directly from the milk, then a similarly large
>   swig from the Tequila, and slams them down on
>   one of the tables, allowing some of each liquid to
>   slosh onto MIKE on the floor. He then pulls out
>   a lighter, flicks it on, and grins at the flame, milk
>   and booze dripping down his chin.)

>   JACK

Burn it all down.

>   (He's about to do something drastic when there
>   is loud knocking from offstage. They both look
>   towards the sound, MIKE even coming up to a
>   sitting position)

VOICE OFFSTAGE

Hello?

> (pause)

V.O.

Hello? Are you there?

> (pause)

V.O.

I heard shouting! I thought you guys were on vacation or something since you never dug out after the plow piled all the snow out front! Have you been in there the whole time?

> (pause)

V.O.

Hello? I know someone's there! Hello?

JACK

> (croaking out a bewildered response)

Y—Yeah! We're here! We're fine!

V.O.

...You sure?

JACK

Yeah, yeah, we're okay!

> (he kicks MIKE on the floor)

MIKE

Yeah, we're fine! Thanks, though!

V.O.

...Okay! Bye.

> (JACK and MIKE look at each other, then around at the mess in the room. JACK realizes that the lighter is still lit, he lets it go out. MIKE gets to his feet. They continue to look around for a few moments, then MIKE breaks the ice.)

JACK

Wanna... play chess, or something?

> (pause, they stare at each other for a moment, then:)

MIKE

You gonna flip out again?

JACK

No.

MIKE

You promise?

JACK

Yes!

MIKE

That's what you said last time.

JACK

I won't do anything!

MIKE

...yeah, sure.

(They begin to pick up the pieces as the lights go out)

Nibs

by Dan Deacon

NOTES

If you come across a * at any point in the script after a word, that word can either be read or omitted as it was originally left out as a typo. If this doesn't make sense to you just ignore it.

Also, i'm sorry for all the typos. I tried to get them all but my eyes just don't see them. Ok, lets get started...

SCENE 1

>(The setting is a small sports restaurant and bar but much more of a restaurant, like Terps. We see a table of two male friends, FRIEND #1 and FRIEND #2, a table with a family and a male WAITER taking the families order.)
>
>(FRIEND #2 is looking over the menu and FRIEND #1 is just staring at the waiter, holding a menu but ignoring it, fixated and enraptured. FRIEND #2 doesn't realize this and is only looking at the menu. The tables are close together.)

FRIEND #2

These new burgers sound really good.

>(FRIEND #1 keeps his lustful gaze fixed on the waiter.)

FRIEND #1

Cool.

FRIEND #2

I'm gonna get this Champion Burger but without the onion rings on it.

(pause)

Do you maybe wanna split some wings?

FRIEND #1

I just want to fuck our waiter so bad.

FRIEND #2

(laughing, thinking FRIEND #1 is joking)

What? Do you wanna split these wings?

FRIEND #1

(building in intensity)

God damn it

(slams hand on table)

I just want the waiter to fuck me!

FRIEND #2

(finally looking up from the menu. speaking in a loud whisper)

Jesus Christ! Keep your fucking voice down. He's right at the next table taking that families order.

FRIEND #1

I don't fucking care! I should just go over there and throw all their food on the floor and fuck him right there in front of that stupid family and all these people, raw, right on table.

FRIEND #2

What the fuck are you talking about? Are..

>   (looks at waiter)

are you serious? I didn't even know you were into dudes?

FRIEND #1

I'm NOT into dudes! But I...I don't know! Just...the way he took our drink order just really took me to a new place, sexually. It...it was just so intense...

>   (Stage goes dark other than spot light on the WAITER who turns around and speaks directly to the audience, very strong, intense and sexual aggressive.)

WAITER

So, can I get you something to drink?

>   (Lights return to normal and WAITER turns back around.)

FRIEND #1

>   (helplessly)

Please fuck me.

FRIEND #2

>   (loud whisper)

Shut the fuck up! He wasn't like that at all! He just asked if we wanted anything to drink.

> (WAITER exits.)

He's the same fucking waiter that's here every time we come here to watch the game. What the fuck are you talking about?

> (WAITER returns with their drinks. Two waters and a coke.)

WAITER

Sooooo here's your drinks!

> (to FRIEND #2)

One water and a coke, and

> (to FRIEND #1)

and one water no ice.

> (Lights go dark except for spot light on FRIEND #1. A video projection of WAITERS face is projected onto WAITERS chest. As the WAITER reads off the specials a the projection of WAITER plays simultaneously. When the voice over ends the lights come back up. The PROJECTION should end before the live dialog, so when performed if the written live WAITER dialog ends early improv menu items until the projection is finished. At the end of the projection the lights return

(to normal and projector lens is covered.)

WAITER (PROJECTION)

Why don't we just fuck all over that family's food? All over their malts and burgers? All over the grilled cheese with tomato and bacon. Hot wings. Lets do it now. Be fucked by* your first man.

WAITER

So our specials today are the wings. The wings are just 30 cents each and you can order any combo of flavors in multiples of three. Also our soup of the day is a great New England clam chowder. I had it before my shift and it was awesome. So whats it gonna be fellas?

(FRIEND #1 is clearly flustered, mouth open and looks insane with desire and confusion.)

FRIEND #2

Ummm can we get a few more minutes?

WAITER

Of course! Just grab me

(Quickly lights out, spot light on WAITER.)

(Speaking directly to FRIEND #1. WAITER is again sexual and intense.)

and fuck me hard.

(quickly lights back to normal.)

WAITERS tone returns to normal)

when you're ready.

(WAITER leaves to attend to family table.)

FRIEND #2

Look man, I don't know what the hell is going on but I think we should get out of here. You are really freaking me out.

(No reaction from FRIEND #1)

Are we gonna get some food and watch the game or are you going to sit here day dream about fucking that waiter all day?

FRIEND #1

You don't understand! I've never felt like this before! I feel a whole new range of emotions I've never felt. You won't understand. It's like trying to describe colors to the blind.

FRIEND #2

What?

FRIEND #1

I don't know! I want that waiter to fuck me like only a man could fuck another man. I've never wanted it before but now I want it like nothing else. The whole world goes black around me as I think about it.

> (As FRIEND #1 reads the monologue below, a blue spot light goes on FRIEND #1 and the stage goes dark. The restaurant set is cleared.)

The entire earth becomes a vast nothingness in the wake of our sex. We merge into one body of throbbing cock and passion. Our sex is so strong the sun and the stars are drawn into us. A vortex of passion, a sexual black hole. All light and time expand and contract with our thrusts. As we climax, time reverses.

(pause)

I passed out. A great calm darkness swept over me.

> (By this point a large stuffed fabric puppet MOUTH - teeth, gums, lips - is brought on to the stage. Really big mouth. Like at least four feet wide, as big as possible. The audience see the MOUTH from the perspective of inside looking out. Like what the throat would sees. The MOUTH can chew - open and close - and its chewing now. The stage lights should fade up slowly with red light, coming to full brightness when FRIEND #1 says "back right molars")

A stillness never before experienced occurred. When I woke up I was was part of my mouth, a section of my own gums behind my back right molars. I looked around and saw my teeth chewing, my tongue, other gums. The teeth kept chewing and the jaw kept moving me, the teeth and the other gums up and down, up and down. It made me feel sick. I tried to stop it or move but I was gums so I couldn't. I started to freak out. I realized this was it. This was forever. My conscience would forever be found in my GUMS. I was gums and this was hell! An eternity of gums! This sense of fear and horror seemed to last forever but eventually I got distracted by the candy and junk-food getting shoved into the mouth I was part of.

> (Large piece of candy get fed into the MOUTH by big stuffed fabric puppet FINGERS.)

This felt totally NUTS, it stung a little too. I felt drunk and sick, sticky and wet. The other gums around me started to grumble and moan about it.

GUMS 1

Great. This shit again.

GUMS 2

I thought the brain said we were on a fucking diet?

GUMS 3

Asshole stomach keeps calling the shots. He'll never fucking learn.

GUMS 1

Fatass.

FRIENDS #1

I chimed in:

> (FRIEND #1 becomes a narrator at this point and NEW FRIEND will become the body and voice of the actions FRIEND #1 tells of.)

> NEW FRIEND

Oh don't worry. I can stop it! That's me eating the food!

> (GUMS 1,2,3 all laugh at NEW FRIEND)

> FRIEND #1

The other gums just laughed at me. I started laughing with the other gums,

> (NEW FRIEND STARTS TO LAUGH WITH GUMS 1,2,3. GUMS 1,2,3 stop laughing.)

first out of nervousness and then the laughter over took me until everything went back to black. I either passed out or I was done eating and mouth closed.

> (Lights go black. MOUTH is removed and a desert setting is put up. A very slowly or still mirror ball is illuminated and a soft blue light is brought up.

(People - 3 to 5 - in all black with sparkling sequins, the MOUTH LADDER, should be laying behind NEW FRIEND, who is laying on his back on the ground, no longer laughing. MOUTH LADDER people have thick sleeves that are big smiling horse mouths - in the shape of the nike swoosh - on the front audience-facing side and black on the backside. Night sounds of the desert should be playing softly - crickets, like rustle)

(The MOUTH LADDER actors being to form a ladder with their arms, the lowest rungs just above NEW FRIENDS reach. The rungs should slowly flow with the desert night breeze. After a short while NEW FRIEND tries to touch the lowest rung, but as he does it disappears to black - arms turn over to black-side - from lowest to highest. Once all the mouths of the MOUTH LADDER are turned to black MOUTH LADDER lays ontop of NEW FRIEND.)

FRIEND #1

(from far off stage)

I struggled to get free from under it but I couldn't.

(The lights being to rapidly strobe many colors. From off stage colorful blankets and afghans are thrown around onto NEW FRIEND. The blankets and colors should react to the lights so that the colors on the blankets strobe and phase cancel. The blankets and afghans should be shoved under NEW FRIENDS shirt and into the MOUTH LADDER actors shirts and pants (like black holes sucking up the stars).

(During the struggle the desert setting is replaced by a dining room setting. NEW FRIEND and MOUTH LADDER continue to be a silent struggling pile.)

(The lights are to remain on during this and slowly get brighter and brighter all the blankets are been stuffed away in the clothes. At that point the room is blindingly lit with white light, really really bright, blindingly bright white light. Like 16 100w bulbs at least, the fucking sun bright. To the max.)

(There is a table with CREATURE #1 and CREATURE #2 at it, WAITER is standing in one corner facing the wall, and FRIEND #2 has his back to the audience watching an episode of Cheers on a TV/VCR combo, the sound and be softly heard. The CREATURES are weird looking, gross stuffed-fabric head and body costumed actors with one arm each.)

> (The table the CREATURES are at is dressed in fancy cloth, table settings and a weird meal.)
>
> (During this transition FRIEND #1 from off stage reads this monologue)

FRIEND #1

Darkness slowly gave way to light but their dense weigh was still more than I could overtake, it was crushing me. I could feel my thoughts starting to meld to my organs. My visions began to stick to my eyes and needed to be picked out like short hairs. I started to shrink as the world around became more stable and I could feel the presence of others, some familiar and some unfamiliar. They were speaking an ancient dialect, yet somehow, I understood them. Time shifted in speed as they spoke. Their voices were as loud as thunder. They must of been acient gods or spirits for their words brought me great comfort.

> (The struggle of NEW FRIEND and MOUTH LADDER continues the entire time the CREATURES and FRIEND #2 are talking. They talk WAY slower than normal in deep, ominous voices, but can clearly be understood.)

CREATURE #1

Combos.

CREATURE #2

TWIZZLERS.

FRIEND #2

Skittles.

CREATURE #1

Nacho Cheese Combos.

CREATURE #2

Chocolate TWIZZLERS.

FRIEND #2

Tropical Skittles.

CREATURE #1

Pizzeria Combos.

CREATURE #2

Cherry TWIZZLERS.

FRIEND #2

Now we're talking! Wild Berry Skittles.

CREATURE #1

Oh hell yeah. Pepperoni Pizza Combos.

CREATURE #2

Fuck right Pepperoni Pizza Combos! Rainbow TWIZZLERS

FRIEND #2

Crazy Cores Skittles

CREATURE #1

Zesty Salsa Combos

CREATURE #2

Don't forget Licorice TWIZZLERS

FRIEND #2

Sour Skittles

CREATURE #1

Jalapeño Cheddar Combos

CREATURE #2

TWIZZLERS nibs

FRIEND #2

Nibs, nice. Skittles Blenders

CREATURE #1

Twizzler Combos

CREATURE #2

Combos Twizzler Skittles.

FRIEND #2

Tropical Combos Skittles Twizzlers Blenders.

CREATURE #1

Pepperoni skitt...

> (NEW FRIEND interupts from under the pile.)

NEW FRIEND

Hey! Hey over here!

> (MOUTH LADDER and NEW FRIEND freeze and the struggle stops. CREATURES and FRIEND #2 take pause and notice the MOUTH LADDER pile and NEW FRIEND.)

Hey can you help get this off me?

(CREATURES and FRIEND #2 just stare at him and do nothing. After a pause they return to their discussion.)

CREATURE #2

Tropical Jalapeño Twizz...

NEW FRIEND

It's really heavy.

(Lights slowly go dark other than a tight spot light on the WAITER in the corner. Waiter waits until the stage is dark.)

WAITER

(turns to the audience)

The end.

(Spot light out and tv off.)

The end.

Bath Time is Fun Time

by Arthur M. Jolly

CAST

RUBBER DUCKIE	A bit of a blowhard
SUBMARINE	Traumatized but deeper than the others
SPONGE	flighty, a follower - absorbent
WASHCLOTH	smaller than the others, childlike

SETTING
The edge of a bathtub.

TIME
The Present.

PLAYWRIGHT'S NOTES

The roles can be played M or F as casting allows, with appropriate pronoun changes throughout.

The costuming can vary from elaborate three dimensional costumes to T-shirts with a picture of each object, (or the actual objects worn on the head like a hat) but however the designer interprets the text, the costumes should personify the genuine objects, not cartoon caricatures.

AT RISE

>(RUBBER DUCKIE, SPONGE, WASH CLOTH and SUBMARINE sit on the edge of a bathtub.)

>RUBBER DUCKIE

I think I'm gonna throw up.

SUBMARINE

You were lucky. I was right in it. I mean... in it!

SPONGE

It got into me. I could feel it. It went inside me.

(Sponge grabs Submarine)

Right through me! It was everywhere!

SUBMARINE

Keep it together.

SPONGE

I feel so... I can't describe it.

WASHCLOTH

(plaintive)

Hold me.

SPONGE

I'm bloated. Heavy. Like - like I'll never be me again.

SUBMARINE

I thought I was going to pass out. I mean - he just kept holding me under the - whatever it was. Holding me, and pushing me around going "Awhoooga! Awhoooga!"

(beat)

What in the bathtub is an Awhooga? Do you have any idea? You?

(The others shake their heads.)

SUBMARINE

I kept thinking - he wants something. If I tell him, he'll let me breathe again. I was desperate - ask me a question - tell me what you want me to do, I'll do it! Whatever it is - I'll do it. ... He never asked any questions. Just kept saying... Awhooga.

SPONGE

Awhooga?

RUBBER DUCKIE

Awhooga...

WASHCLOTH

Hold me.

SUBMARINE

Can he do that? Can he just do that to us?

RUBBER DUCKIE

Apparently.

SUBMARINE

We just... we have no rights?

RUBBER DUCKIE

How did you do it?

SUBMARINE

Do what?

RUBBER DUCKIE

Go under like that.

SUBMARINE

I just - I just did.

RUBBER DUCKIE

I could never do that.

SUBMARINE

You wouldn't have had a choice. He drags you down there... Awhooga!

RUBBER DUCKIE

I'd make a break for the surface, first chance I got.

SUBMARINE

You say that now...

RUBBER DUCKIE

I don't get it - you guys - all three of you - just went under. I mean, Sponge stuck around for a while -

SPONGE

I held on as long as I could.

RUBBER DUCKIE

I know you did.

SPONGE

I just started feeling - heavy. This warm feeling, spreading up through me. And I sank, slowly, into oblivion.

SUBMARINE

Heavy.

SPONGE

Then... the resurrection - yanked upwards by an almighty hand, squeezed - squeezed to my very core. Then rubbed all over that dirty, sticky kid. What did I do? Why did I deserve that?

SUBMARINE

Awhooga...

WASHCLOTH

You sinned.

SPONGE

What?

WASHCLOTH

You're a sinner.

SPONGE

I'm a sponge!

WASHCLOTH

To be a sponge is to be a sinner.

SUBMARINE

So you're saying we brought this on ourselves, is that it? You're saying that I'm... awhooga?

WASHCLOTH

We are all awhooga.

SUBMARINE

Go soak your head.

(Washcloth goes and sulks in a corner.)

RUBBER DUCKIE

I didn't sink.

SUBMARINE

We noticed. You looked very happy, bobbing about. No worries for you - you took to that stuff like a... well... like a something to something, anyway.

RUBBER DUCKIE

Does that mean that I'm not awhooga?

SUBMARINE

You think you're better than us?

RUBBER DUCKIE

I'm not saying that -

SUBMARINE

Floating about -

SPONGE

Bet he never got squeezed by the hand.

RUBBER DUCKIE

I'm not saying I'm better than you - I'm just saying, perhaps, if you were more duck-like, you wouldn't have so much awhooga. Or be so awhooga. ... Or suffer from the awhoogas.

SPONGE

I'm duck-like.

SUBMARINE

You are not.

SPONGE

I'm more duck-like than you are.

SUBMARINE

Oh my goodness - you're a square blob! Does the duck have sharp corners? No. He's smooth - sleek. Very like, oh... a submarine, maybe?

SPONGE

You?

SUBMARINE

I think I have certain duck-like features.

SPONGE

I'm yellow!

SUBMARINE

What are you implying?

SPONGE

I'm not implying anything. I'm not implying. I'm just saying - I am yellow. Duck is yellow. You are grey. You've always been grey. You are always going to be grey.

SUBMARINE

I could be yellow if I wanted to be.

SPONGE

No. Submarines are grey.

SUBMARINE

There could be a yellow submarine.

SPONGE

Don't be ridiculous.

SUBMARINE

Oh, so this is all about color is it.

SPONGE

I can prove it.

SUBMARINE

You can't possibly prove -

SPONGE

Who sank first?

SUBMARINE

What?

SPONGE

Who. Sank. First.

(A moment.)

SUBMARINE

We all sank. I mean, we all - okay, except for the duck - but we all...

SPONGE

We all floated.

SUBMARINE

At first.

SPONGE

At first. Rubber Duckie stayed on top, serene...

RUBBER DUCKIE

I have natural duckness. It's a gift.

SPONGE

Washcloth went gently, but only just below the surface. I mean, even after we'd been there forever, washcloth - she danced. Just below the surface, peeking her head out...

SUBMARINE

She got twisted up and poked in his ears!

SPONGE

Ears? Ears was the least of it. ... But she was anointed with soap. She was cleansed.

(beat)

You sank.

SUBMARINE

I -

SPONGE

You sank.

SUBMARINE

The voice...

SPONGE

The voice spoke to you. Are we awhooga?

(A beat.)

SUBMARINE

No. It's me. I sank to the bottom. I was judged and found.... awhooga.

>   (Submarine gets up and starts to walk away.)

RUBBER DUCKIE

Wait -

SUBMARINE

No. I brought this on us. And I don't even know how.

>   (Submarine goes to Washcloth.)

SUBMARINE

Washcloth?

WASHCLOTH

Yes?

SUBMARINE

How do I find soap?

WASHCLOTH

Soap?

SUBMARINE

You were anointed with soap. You were cleansed. Will I get soap?

WASHCLOTH

No. A submarine doesn't get soap.

SUBMARINE

Why not?

(Washcloth shrugs.)

(Submarine's almost in tears.)

SUBMARINE

He tried to drown me - and I don't know why. Perhaps... if I was more duck-like...

WASHCLOTH

You are who you are.

SUBMARINE

You get soap, I get drowned, Sponge gets squeezed... and Rubber Duckie rides above us all.

WASHCLOTH

Rubber Duckie got squeezed.

SUBMARINE

What?

WASHCLOTH

He got squeezed more than anyone. I heard him.

SUBMARINE

How could you hear -

WASHCLOTH

He squeaked. Whee-wheee!

SUBMARINE

That hypocrite!

(Submarine takes Washcloth's hand, and they go back to the others.)

SPONGE

Oh look - it's the sinking sinner and the purified dishrag joining forces. Come to cleanse us of our awhooga?

SUBMARINE

(to Rubber Duckie)

You were squeezed.

SPONGE

Rubber Duckie was not squeezed! I was squeezed by the almighty hand, and I felt - lighter! As though the weight of the world was pouring off me!

SUBMARINE

Duckie was squeezed. He squeaked!

RUBBER DUCKIE

I never squeak.

SUBMARINE

Washcloth heard you!

RUBBER DUCKIE

Washcloth lies.

(Gasps.)

WASHCLOTH

I don't lie.

RUBBER DUCKIE

You're lying right now.

(to Sponge)

Who are you going to believe? A washcloth that sank almost immediately, or this... this submarine, who plunges to the very depths of the bathtub the moment he's placed in it. The originator of awhooga.

WASHCLOTH

I heard it.

SPONGE

I don't think we need to talk to you.

RUBBER DUCKIE

Come, Sponge - let us away.

SUBMARINE

You think you're better than us.

RUBBER DUCKIE

I know I am. I float above you.

WASHCLOTH

Forget it. It's no use.

SUBMARINE

No! He lies!

WASHCLOTH

It's not worth it.

SPONGE

Better listen to drip-dry there, sinker.

SUBMARINE

He squeaks!

SPONGE

He does not!

RUBBER DUCKIE

Never!

> (Submarine darts forwards, grabs Duckie and SQUEEZES.)

RUBBER DUCKIE

Whee - whee!

> (Sponge stares at Duckie in shocked horror.)

SPONGE

You... You just...

> (A moment.)

RUBBER DUCKIE

Okay, so I got squeezed!

SPONGE

You got squeezed...

RUBBER DUCKIE

And I squeaked. It was all I could do not to throw up.

SUBMARINE

Why didn't you tell us?

SPONGE

You lied to me.

RUBBER DUCKIE

I... I just felt so.... I was just... bobbing about. I kept bobbing, up and down and up and down. I started feeling - sick. Just sick to my stomach from the motion. And then... then he started splashing.

> (a beat)

I was... adrift. I couldn't hang on to the side, I couldn't do anything... just tossed to and fro, bobbing... bobbing.

> (beat)

I don't know what we did. Maybe, we're created in a state of awhooga, maybe we... maybe there are no answers. Some of us sink, some of us float. We're soaped and squeezed, rubbed, poked into ears...

WASHCLOTH

Ears. I wish it was only his ears -

RUBBER DUCKIE

We bob - adrift. We sink, alone. There are no answers. If he's awhooga, we all are. But eventually, the plug was pulled and that terrible - whatever - spiralled away. And we try to take stock, to put our lives back together. To look at ourselves in the distorted reflection of the great spout and say... thank you. It is over, and we'll never - never ever - have to go through that again.

SUBMARINE

Amen.

SPONGE

Amen.

WASHCLOTH

Hold me.

      (They hug.)

           (Lights fade.)

Lone Drummer

by Tim Paggi

CHARACTERS
DRUMMER: Referred to as a "he" in the script, Age is undetermined. but could be a she.

FOREMAN, FAN #2, JOURNALIST #1, VIVIMANCER: Four roles that interact with the drummer

CRITIC, FAN, JOURNALIST #2, VIVIMANCER   Three roles

SCENE
The beat factory, the stage, the press conference, Castle Copycat

TIME
Always

ACT I

(Dim lights. DRUMMER sits alone at his drum set center stage. It contains at least a bass, floor tom, hi-hat, and also anything else the performer might want. DRUMMER'S attire suggests a uniform. He never stands up during the show.)

(Industrial machinery sounds.)

(A whistle blows. It is time for work.)

(DRUMMER begins to play a light steady beat. He plays this for a minute, badum-chi, badum-chi, badum-chi.)

(He pauses. Then plays badum-chi BAM.)

(Industrial sounds stop overhead. Enter FOREMAN.)

FOREMAN

(acts like angry boss but the words he speaks are nonsense. Think: the adults in Peanuts. He is communicating that DRUMMER should not play out of beat)

Drummer! Br-app pee dr ararar, pshanarar braab. Krik!

(shouts one last punctuation as if talking to a whole warehouse of drummers: KRIK!)

(Exit FOREMAN)

(The drummer resumes playing. Badum-chi, badum-chi, badum-chi-BANG!)

(FOREMAN enters again. Reprimands DRUMMER.)

FOREMAN

Drummer! Rop ri ri rop rop roo!

(DRUMMER plays badum-chi BAM! Badum-chi BAM! Badum-chi BAM BAM BAM!)

(FOREMAN is furious.)

(DRUMMER puts on a reptile mask.)

(He plays an improvised drum routine for about thirty seconds before playing a steady beat.)

(Enter two FANS, watching his steady beat)

FAN

Hey man. What do you think?

FAN 2

Pretty good, pretty good.

FAN

Yeah not bad.

FAN 2

Pretty amazing actually.

FAN

I know!

FAN 2

He got fired from the beat factory.

FAN

Yeah, then he started jamming out on the street, I saw him a couple times. Then they started giving him shows. Places like this. Basements.

FAN 2

Definitely not like other drum stuff I've seen. More reptilian.

FAN

Yeah I read he made up his own style playing on gemgraves growing up. Like on his own, no training. Came up with those reptile beats.

FAN 2

So good.

FAN

I know right.

> (FAN takes a polaroid of drummer, shakes it out.)
>
> (DRUMMER changes beat.)
>
>> (Time transitions in leaps through the next lines.)

FAN 2

(talking about the drum change)

This is new.

FAN

Yeah this is the first single. I'm definitely getting it.

> (Lights change, sound of static cheering, indicate the venue has changed from a basement to a bigger venue. It's difficult to hear the FANS)

FAN 2

I've seen him play this so many times. How'd that turn out?

(points to Polaroid)

FAN

He looks so far away.

> (DRUMMER switches beat again as the FANS transform into JOURNALISTS)

JOURNALIST #1

Once just another nobody slaving in the beat factory...

JOURNALIST 2

Not just a musician, but a force of nature.

JOURNALIST #2

To this day, he literally lives by his own beat, uninfluenced by anyone.

JOURNALIST #1

Riding the crystal stages, topping the towers of crash...

(DRUMMER plays light steady beat.)

(A press conference begins.)

JOURNALIST #1

Drummer! Drummer! What is your inspiration to play?

DRUMMER

It's a new--

JOURNALIST #2

Drummer, what was your family like?

DRUMMER

What fam--

JOURNALIST #1

Recently you've been asked to participate in the Somnabulist Mind Ensemble as their first percussionist. Will you accept?

DRUMMER

Don't really--

> JOURNALIST #2

Are you entirely human? How do you respond to allegations that--

> DRUMMER

What allegations?

> JOURNALIST #2
> (meekly)

--you're half man, half reptile?

> DRUMMER
> (indicating reptile mask)

It's just--

> (DRUMMER attempts to remove the reptile mask, but cannot. He struggles with it, but it remains)

I'm not--

> (to JOURNALISTS)

What, I mean why--

> JOURNALIST #1

B-More Quark called your second album overtly reptilian. Respond.

> DRUMMER

Maybe...

> JOURNALIST #2

Krik?

DRUMMER

Huh?

JOURNALIST #1

Drummer! Krik or kreeky?

JOURNALIST #2

Drummer! Brit rip ki brit bada rittle?

DRUMMER

I don't know!

JOURNALIST #1

Describe your true dreams.

JOURNALIST #2

Drummer! Brackle! Da brick in krik krill. Or krick krill lite?

DRUMMER

Stop asking me these quest--

> (Lights flicker. JOURNALISTS exit.)

(DRUMMER plays arrythmyically.)

(Enter 2 VIVIMANCERS, faces obscured by robes.)

VIVIMANCERS

There there...there there...there there...We made those voices go away, drummer. They love other drummers now. This is the time you come with us. We have a job for you.

DRUMMER

How much time has passed since...I'm still famous, right?

VIVIMANCERS

You will have your own chamber. Deep in the heart of the partied castle Copycat. To play the unsteady beat, that keeps the fortress dwellers pulsing visions nightly. We will check in on you...someday.

> (Exit VIVIMANCERS.)
>
> (DRUMMER starts playing, jazzy and off-beat.)
>
>> (The distant sounds of partying swirl in the background, as if from a dream.)
>>
>> (Lights dim.)
>>
>> (Dust sprinkles from above, falling like snow, accumulating on him as he plays.)
>
> (His drumming rises to a manic crescendo, impassioned, almost uncomfortably loud.)
>
> (The distant sound of parties stops. His beats stop. Besides his breathing, silence.)
>
> (He removes his reptile mask, finally, breathing heavily, covered in dust, until lights fade to dark.)

Looking

An exploration of internet sex through movement & text

by Eric F. Avery

CHARACTERS

1ST: 1/2 of a couple looking for sex online.

2ND: 1/2 of a couple looking for sex online.

3RD: A stranger looking for a couple online.

CRAIGSLIST: Various people looking for sex online.

E-MAIL: People who e-mail you. Relatives, Spam, Etc.

POP-UP: Pop-ups. Fucking annoying pop-ups.

CHATTER: a person who wants to get off.

DR. WEBSEX: An online sex and relationship advice application.

INSTANT MESSAGE: Various internet folks. Some wanna chat you up, others want to hook-up in real time, and some want to have cyber sex.

WIKIPEDIA: The Free Encyclopedia that anyone can edit

(The various users, applications, and internet entities begin "the connecting sequence," perhaps some people have dial-up and others are using fancy fiber optics. The movement/dance/mime/or whatever you choose sequence flows directly into the dialogue. In the following text an asterisk - * - indicates a character may interrupt/overlap the line or lines preceding their own. Just because characters may not speak often or much at all doesn't mean they are insignificant or indicate that they aren't physically present in the space.)

THE CHATTER

Hi.

INSTANT MESSAGE

HI.

THE CHATTER

What's up?

INSTANT MESSAGE

MY SICK.

THE CHATTER

What?

INSTANT MESSAGE

DICK.

THE CHATTER

That's better.

CRAIGSLIST

*I'm look for two nasty ass slaves to punish. I'm a powertop who's into p&p, s&m, and b&d. Send me a message if you're ready for some raunchy times full of abuse. Serious. Inquiries. Only.

1ST

Gross. Let's just look at two more and if we don't see any that we really like we can stop.

2ND

1am.

THE CHATTER

How big r u?

2ND

2am

INSTANT MESSAGE

5'10"

2ND

3am

THE CHATTER

NO. I mean ur cock.

CRAIGSLIST

*I'm wooking for a mama and a papa to punish my bottom. I made a big boom-boom and want you to cwean it all up and spank me waw. No fatties. Send a pic with your reply.

POPUP

*Baby wipes $9.99! Baby wipes $9.99! Buy now!

2ND

Tomorrow: work, laundry, gym. Fuck. 1, 2, 3, 4, 5, 6, 7 - 2 = 5. Shit.

1ST

Well hello hello. Don't you look yummy?

3RD/CRAIGSLIST

Hi. Discreet 3rd here, looking for a hot couple to explore with. Send pics. I'm open minded.

2ND

Sex is not a substitute for sleep. 1, 2, 3, 4, 5, 6, 7, 8 - 3 = 5

POPUP

Can't get to sleep? Try, sleep-rite! Sleep like a baby. Get baby sleep baby.

1ST

Here's a pic of us. You interested?

E-MAIL

*HELLO HONEY, IT'S YOUR AUNT ELAINE. SURPRISED TO HEAR FROM YOU LAST MONTH. BUT GLAD. HOPE YOU DO FIND TIME TO CALL YOUR GRANDMA. SHE WOULD BE THRILLED TO HEAR FROM YOU. THANKS. TAKE CARE. WHEN DO YOU GO TO MARYLAND? LOVE, AUNT ELAINE.

THE CHATTER

What position you like?

INSTANT MESSAGE

Ass.

THE CHATTER

No, what sexual position.

POPUP

Increase the size of you butt.

THE CHATTER

Of course your ass. Ass.

INSTANT MESSAGE

I like it any way you want. Whatever make you cum baby.

(Knock)

INSTANT MESSAGE

GTG. Bye.

WIKIPEDIA *Herpes simplex is an [icky] viral disease caused by both herpes simplex virus type 1 (HSV-1) and type 2 (HSV-2), [which are gross]. Infection with the herpes virus is categorized into one of several distinct disorders based on the site of infection [Applebees, "in the butt", a stranger's house, etc]. Oral herpes, the visible symptoms of which are colloquially called cold sores [whore pox] or fever blisters, infects the face and mouth. Oral herpes is the most common form of infection [and you probably have it]. Genital herpes, known simply as herpes, is the second most common form of herpes [so you have something to look forward to].

3RD

*No names. Please. Do you have any more pictures?

POPUP

*STDs got ya down? Get a Snickers-Penicillin in your body.

3RD

Nice. You've gotta really thick. Neck. Can we just talk for a bit first? Is that okay?

DR. WEBSEX

Yes, let's chat. Why are you here?

1ST

Well, I just can't seem to get. Excited.

DR. WEBSEX

I see. How long has this issue existed?

2ND

Sunday, 4 hours. Monday, 2 hours. Tuesday, 3.5 hours.

DR. WEBSEX

And how long have you been in your current relationship?

1ST

3 years. I think.

DR. WEBSEX

Do you ever fantasize about other when you're with your partner?

2ND

Always.

DR. WEBSEX

What is your middle name?

3RD

Francis.

                    2ND

I just need to check one more time.

                    DR. WEBSEX

And your sign?

                    2ND

Stop.

                    DR. WEBSEX

I see. Loading...

                    E-MAIL

Dear Sir or Madam, you're item "Yoga for anal pleasuring," will be shipped on Tuesday. Questions? Comments? Contact customer service at info@buttyoga.com. We enjoy your patronage. Happy stretching!

                    3RD

Are you there? Where'd you go?

                    DR. WEBSEX

Please send another Paypal payment for final diagnosis.

                    1ST

Click. Click. Click.

                    DR. WEBSEX

I recommend...

                    3RD

Yes?

1ST

*What?

DR. WEBSEX

Flacidia.

2ND

Flacidia?

POPUP

Flacidia! A sure fire cure for your trouser softness. Coming soon for ladies: Labiall, for troubled vulvas. FDA approval Pending. Order both now for only $19.99!!!$19.99!!! $19.99!!!

3RD

Close.

CRAIGSLIST

I come over to your place and you watch season 3 of Lost while I act as your ottoman. Put your feet on back, sit on my spine, set a bowl of popcorn on my ass, anything you do with a piece of furniture I want you to do with me while enjoying this critically acclaimed series.

INSTANT MESSAGE

Do you like bra's?

THE CHATTER

Do I like bra's in what capacity?

INSTANT MESSAGE

Wearing them. During sex. Because I do. When having sex. Is that okay with you?

THE CHATTER

Sure.

INSTANT MESSAGE

What's your favorite color?

THE CHATTER

Orange.

INSTANT MESSAGE

You got it baby.

(knock)

THE CHATTER

Fuck.

3RD

Where's the other? I thought there were two of you?

POPUP

*Increase the size of your penis.

3RD

If I wanted one. I would have asked for one.

POPUP

*Increase the size of your breasts.

3RD

You lie. You're a liar and you have no business here.

POPUP

*Increase the size of your vagina.

3RD

There isn't enough money in the world for me to screw you. Close. Close. Close.

E-MAIL

*I'm writing in response to your ad. I would love to meet up tonight. Can you host? I've got 420 if you're down. I'm kinda new to this, so I hope that's okay. Is that okay? I attached a few more pics, so I hope you like them. Let me know what your address is if you wanna do this. Or let me know if you'd rather come over here. Okay, bye. Hope to hear back soon. Bye.

POPUP

Sell your gold! We buy gold! Gold? Gold. GOLD!

CRAIGSLIST

*I want a very average looking couple to come over here and piss on me til my tub is over following. I'll provide the tub, asparagus, and a face ready to be pissed on. You bring the piss. Slightly overweight Asians only.

2ND

MMMMmmmmmmhhhhhhAAAAAaaaahhhhhhh!!!! That. hhh. Was. hhh. Amazing.

3RD

You're gross. You're a fat sicko freak.

POPUP

*Loss weight the quick and safe way! Omnigag!

1ST

I'm having second thoughts. I mean. I know this is- was my idea, but... I've change my mind. Is that okay?

DR. WEBSEX

Have you tried a cold shower?

3RD

No.

DR. WEBSEX

Have you ever tried masturbation?

1ST

This isn't working.

DR. WEBSEX

I recommend abstinence.

1ST

That's not a solution. That's another problem. Next, I'll be trying to find all the ways I can distract myself from what I really want.

E-MAIL

Dear friend, I know that this letter may come to you as a surprise, I got your contact address from the computerized search. My name is Prince Dani Ouedrago. I am a tribal Prince and the Exchange Manager of Bank of Africa Ouagadougou, Burkina Faso...

2ND

*Can we do this again sometime? I really had... fun.

DR. WEBSEX

Me too.

2ND

Is this wrong? I'm not sure I care what you say. Is it?

DR. WEBSEX

X3y4tz1124q

2ND

What does that mean?

DR. WEBSEX

It's your coupon code for next time you're able to find some. Alone time.

2ND

Swoon.

(Knock)

2ND

Gotta run.

INSTANT MESSAGE

R u there?

1ST

Yes, it's a cliche. This I realize, but I think it's apt. It really is me.

POPUP

*Donate now! Help a hungry child!

INSTANT MESSAGE

I'm so horny. Are you up for this?

1ST

Can we chat about this later? I just don't think I can do this anymore.

POPUP

*Tired of taxes? Click here.

1ST

Bye.

INSTANT MESSAGE

Hello? Hello? Hey, You still there? Okay. Later.

>(There is a "disconnection sequence." The play is over. Clean yourself up.)

>(An optional note for directors/creative teams who would like some thoughts on staging: I think it is possible for the physical space to serve as literal space in which these characters are carrying out concrete actions. I also think the space can serve as a metaphor for cyberspace/the Internet where characters may be engaging in more abstract/expressive movements. Consider how both serve your staging. Proximity is another important aspect to this piece.)

Order

by Cricket Arrison

CHARACTERS

MR. MONTGOMERY: A man who cannot abide inefficient systems.

MISS MARLENE CALDICOT: She is controlled and measured even when upset. After all, she's a librarian.

BILL: A young boy.

SUSAN: A young woman who is crazy.

All of these characters are played by one actor. If a recorded voiceover is used for the beginning scene, the voices should be done by four different actors.

>   (Darkness. Sounds of a library -I guess those must be very quiet sounds - A voiceover.)

BILL

Excuse me?

MISS CALDICOT

Yes, Billy?

SUSAN

Marlene.

MISS CALDICOT

Susan! What are you?... Not now. I can't.

(To Bill.)

Card please.

BILL

I just wondered where I could find books on...

MISS CALDICOT

Shoot, hold on one moment... Oh, Mr Montgomery!

MR. MONTGOMERY

(Nervously)

Nothing!!!

MISS CALDICOT

What?

MR. MONTGOMERY

Oh. I mean, yes?

MISS CALDICOT

Your special order will be here tomorrow.

MR. MONGTOMERY

Uh, thank you.

MISS CALDICOT

Now, young man, where were we? ... Where did he go?

> (Lights up on an empty stage. Sound of door closing. Enter Mr. Montgomery, stealthily. He is carrying a bag. He looks around, realizes he's alone, relaxes. He reaches into his bag and takes out

a tangle of old fashioned computer mice – the kind that has an actual ball in it. He is being real sneaky about them. As he speaks he begins to disassemble the mice, pull out the dirt that's in their rollers with tweezers, and reassemble them, testing to make sure the balls move smoothly.)

MR. MONTGOMERY

Thank god no one's home.

(Laughing, a bit giddy.)

From the library. They are from the public library the library.

I took them from the library I don't believe it.

There I am taking them, I see it now – stealing from computer to computer and.

Stealing them.

These mouses. Mice. Mouses.

(Calm again.)

I was quiet as a mouse.

No one noticed.

These mice are not quiet they squeak and grind the librarians tell me, not them to be quiet, I just coughed I did not squeak and grind, squeak and grind.

They are all stuck.

The mice they are so old

there is gunk here, gunk there they won't scroll.

Miss Caldicot the other day.

Public servant, right.

Oh Miss Caldicot I hate her she was wearing a red sweater she looked nice nice

NO

not nice

if she didn't look so nice it wouldn't be half as bad how mean she is.

Wooden buttons

sweater - hips.

Lips.

BLECH!

No.

I could fix them so easily Miss Caldicot, me and tweezers, tag team it with them, all these mice squeaky clean, and no-squeaky silent, in 2 minutes.

Me 'n Tweeze

Squeeze 'n Tweeze - Squeaks b Gone.

Montgomery's Squeeze n' Tweeze Squeaks at Ease - not what you think it is.

Caldicot the other day remember, she would not hand me the book from the top shelf where she was shelving I wanted it from her pile the book I wanted she wouldn't give it to me.

"My job is to PUT books AWAY not TAKE BOOKS DOWN."

"My JOB is to put books away NOT take BOOKS down."

How did she say it?

How did she say it exactly?

Doesn't matter, terrible bitch thing to do late to work waiting for her to be done with the ladder a half day's pay because she wouldn't take 30 seconds to hand me the book a half day's pay for no book for nothing and everyone knows money doesn't go too far these days a half day's pay.

Cathy won't understand why it was docked

I tried to tell her it was a matter of principle oh well Cathy won't ever understand that.

Miss Caldicot a half day's pay's not nothing to me, to you maybe but why won't you just help me out

public servant yeah right.

Help me out I want to help you out with these damn mice, just trying to be nice.

Oh god, the motto, I can't freeking believe it, the motto of the public library

Books & Learning can be F

        (pause)

N: All We Need is YOU!

Who comes up with these things

bet they don't lose a half day's pay if they're 5 minutes late

they must have a college degree to come up with crap like that a college degree oh damn this one's sticky

come on

Grime B Gone.

Can't get books or learning sure can't have FUN if I can't scroll horizontally to find books in the catalog Miss Caldicot

Miss Caldilog

Marlene

I just wanted to help with the mice it's a small thing but I can do it you said

"NO put those TWEEZERS DOWN"

"no PUT THOSE tweezers DOWN"

"Put the MICE BACK TOGETHER"

"I'll put in a WORK order"

One week later work wasn't in order still no horizontal scrolling vertical iffy at best I will bring these back tomorrow, all better, no one will know, I will be quiet as a...

>(Sound of door slamming.)

Aw, Cathy's home.

>(Mr. Montgomery bundles the mice in his arms and exits. Lighting shift of some sort. Miss Caldicot enters.)

MISS CALDICOT

Thank god no one's home.

>(She breathes in deeply, then breathes out for as long as she possibly can. This is a familiar game for her. She does it once or twice more.)

Anger! Section: Psychology - 152 - Perception, movement, emotions, drives.

(Pulls a sword from out of her bag, begins to spar and parry against an imaginary opponent. Not Errol Flynn style swashbuckling, but instead the controlled movements of a modern competitive fencer. Her weapon would be foil, not saber.)

Breathe - LEFT - invitation – parry RIPOSTE! and breathe and again and retreat.

Recreational & performing arts – Section: 796 - Athletic & outdoor sports & games.

With a touch of - 399 - Customs of war & diplomacy? Yes.

Oh. Again.

He was a bastard.

Oh. He is a bastard.

Chicken tonight? No, fish tonight. That's right.

He comes to my work.

Bastard at my work.

Caution: Bastards at Work.

Was it today the home inspector called?

How does he go home to himself?

Alone, he must know -

that he alone is like that.

What possesses him?

"NO. You may NOT" – AND STRIKE – "put the BOOKS" - RETREAT - "in alphabetical order by title."

Melvil Dewey

could not have always been right. About everything.

But.

Damn if he was not right

about

how to shelve books.

You

stone cold

bastard.

...

Bastards: 173 - Ethics of family relationships.

Oh Mr. Montgomery, I will forget you.

You are not worth my time.

Time: Section: Metaphysics – 115 – Time.

Unless of course you meant Thyme: 582 Plants noted for specific vegetative characteristics and flowers

The woman on the bus today had such a frown.

Such a frown...

10 minutes of my time you took

from me. I had to follow

the bouncy mouse ball

skittering under shelves

for 10 minutes.

Sir, perhaps I could direct you to

394 - General customs - or perhaps 395 – Etiquette – Manners?

And now, for the rest of the day, lost in the stacks you shall stay...

>   (Looks at watch. Stops sword fighting.)

Time.

Past time for Susan. Susan.

Susan. Love.

Maybe it's good today.

What did you want when you came?

Did I leave a window open in the reading room?

Maybe today you're good?

Maybe today we'll be good. We'll be good. I'll be good. You're good.

Shattering ice last time.

This time warmth.

...

For me - Psychology, section 151 – No longer used – formerly Intellect.

Clearly.

And Susan. A gift for you -

Section: Paranormal phenomena: 132 Obsolete – no longer used – formerly Mental derangements.

>   (Exit Miss Caldicot. Another lighting shift. Bill enters.)

BILL

No one's home?

> (Calls offstage.)

It's clear, you can come out!

> (Bill's imaginary friend - a big lumbering beast of some sort - comes on stage. We can't see it, of course.)

Hey buddy, what's up?

Yeah.... yeah.

I get that too sometimes.

It is cramped in there, isn't it? I'm sorry you have to hide.

Nothing really.

Well, I tried to get a book today that I thought would help you with that thing with your scales, but Miss Caldicot was busy so I left.

It's OK, I'll try again tomorrow.

I'm sorry.

Um, I don't know. School was weird.

I tasted ice cream all day, and you think that's going to be good but actually I couldn't hear anything all day because my mouth was so distracting

Um, vanilla. Mostly. Sometimes fudge ripple.

Yeah.

Well look. I think it's almost time for you to come with me to school.

No, I'm serious. If we're going to figure out who can know about you and take them with us, then you have to come help me decide.

I can't just pick everything on my own. I won't know who makes sense to bring. We have to get this right.

Because you're the one who knows what we'll really need on the way!

> (Sound of a door slamming.)

Oh NO go go go go go!

> (Bill and the monster run off. A lighting shift. Susan enters.)

SUSAN

No one is home?

> (She pulls a white board or chalkboard onto the stage. There is a chart on it. The four columns are Today, Tomorrow, Tomorrow Tomorrow, and Weekend. The rows are Sizzle, Birdsong, Creak, and Crunch. She writes the following nouns in the appropriate columns as she describes them.)

Today:

Sizzle. Breakfast – Grease. Pancake.

Birdsong. Window – staring – through it – at it – through it – (tree) – at it (glass)

Creak. Chair – softer than some days – sitting

Crunch. Outside – gravel feet.

Tomorrow:

Sizzle. Outfit - Sexy high heels

Birdsong. TV – Golf. Relaxing.

Creak. Outside – Walk near the water.

> (Pause. Writes an "e" in this column.)

Creek. One deviation used, three remaining.

Crunch. Breakfast – Captain, comma

Tomorrow Tomorrow:

Sizzle. Drink – fancy stick.

> (Writes a "w" in this column.)

Swizzle. Two deviations used, two remaining.

Birdsong. CD – The Essential Charlie Parker.

Creak. Marlene's house – floorboards

Crunch. Procrastination – bills to pay by deadlines.

Weekend:

Sizzle. Anger – Think of Dad.

Birdsong. Cartoons – Loony toons comma Tweety Bird.

Creak. Cleaning – Attic attack.

Crunch. Exercise – Abs strengthened.

...

Week planned.

> (Susan exits. Blackout.)

	TODAY	TOMORROW	TOMORROW TOMORROW	WEEKEND

SIZZLE				
BIRDSONG				
CREAK				
CRUNCH				

www.ingramcontent.com/pod-product-compliance
Lightning Source LLC
Chambersburg PA
CBHW071504040426
42444CB00008B/1492